The Michigan Guide to the ECCE

Developing High-Intermediate Competence in English

VOLUME 1

Fernando Fleurquin

John W. McLaughlin

Amy D. Yamashiro

University of Michigan
English Language Institute

MICHIGAN

ISBN-10: 0-472-03168-6
ISBN-13: 978-0-472-03168-9

Published in the United States of America
The University of Michigan Press
Manufactured in the United States of America

∞ Printed on acid-free paper

2009   2008   2007   2006   4   3   2   1

Contents

Introduction

In making this book, we wanted it to serve several purposes. Rather than simply creating a test preparation book for the Examination for the Certificate of Competence in English (ECCE), we wanted to create a textbook that classroom teachers could use with students that would have engaging readings and topics for discussion and writing. We have organized each unit around general themes that tie together the reading, writing, and speaking activities, and many of the listening activities. Moreover, many of the exercises are designed for small group activities for a more interactive class. While some exercises are closed, many are open-ended and should make for interesting comparisons among students' answers. At the same time, we wanted this book to be useful for students who may use it for self-study. Teachers may also assign exercises for homework as we have provided an ample range of activities in every unit. The mini-tests and the full test follow the ECCE format fairly closely, and the exercises were designed to help you practice features of English that are commonly tested on the ECCE. The book provides practice with all four language skills—listening, speaking, reading, and writing—as well as vocabulary and grammar.

Overview of the ECCE

ECCE is a standardized examination of English as a Foreign Language. It is developed and scored by the Testing Division, English Language Institute of the University of Michigan. It is administered by authorized test centers in a variety of countries. The ECCE tests all four skill areas: listening, speaking, reading, and writing, and evaluates the ability to effectively use standard colloquial English in realistic contexts.

Level of the ECCE

The ECCE emphasizes communicative use of English rather than formal knowledge of the language. It is aimed at examinees who can perform functional and communicative transactions in the four skills: listening, speaking, reading, and writing. The content and difficulty of the ECCE aim at the B2 level of the Common European Framework. The level of the ECCE is similar to the First Certificate in English (FCE), to TOEFL® scores with approximate ranges from 450–525 (paper-based), 150–200 (computer-based), and 50–75 (Internet-based), or to TOEIC® scores with approximate ranges of 500–700. This is usually achieved at high-intermediate or low-advanced courses, depending on the language center.

Main Uses of the ECCE

Students use the ECCE for personal, social, and occupational uses. Schools may integrate the ECCE into their curriculum as external validation of the quality and level of their academic program. Employers may request the ECCE certificate to determine that the candidate has the sufficient proficiency level to perform the job tasks in English.

Format and Content of the ECCE

Test items and tasks are developed to evaluate the four skills. The total time for test administration is approximately 2½ to 3 hours. The four sections of the ECCE are shown in the chart.

Section	Number of Items	Description	Time
Listening	30	Part I (multiple-choice) Each short conversation is followed by a question. Three picture options are shown as answer choices.	30 mins.
	20	Part II (multiple-choice) A radio interview is broken into several segments. Several questions follow each segment. Brief written options are presented as answer choices.	
Grammar, Vocabulary, Reading	35	Grammar (multiple-choice) An incomplete sentence is presented with several options. One answer choice is grammatically correct.	80 mins.
	35	Vocabulary (multiple choice) An incomplete sentence is shown with several answer choices. One option has the correct meaning to complete the sentence.	
	30	Reading (multiple choice) Part I: A short reading passage is followed by comprehension questions. Part II: Short texts are presented as advertisements followed by questions. Part III: Longer related texts are presented like an information brochure and followed by comprehension questions.	
Writing	1 task	A short passage in the form of a news brief, memo, or letter is presented as a writing prompt. Examinees may choose to respond in the form of a letter or essay.	30 mins.
Speaking	4 tasks	A structured oral interaction occurs between the examinee and the oral examiner. The interaction includes a brief interview and the use of a picture prompt.	15 mins.

The speaking section is scored by a trained oral examiner in the local test administration area; the other sections are all scored by the UM-ELI. The listening, reading, and writing sections are administered in this sequence at one time. The speaking test may be given either before or after the three other sections of the test.

Why We Wrote *The Michigan Guide to the ECCE*

This textbook was written in response to the demand for preparation materials for the ECCE. The book serves two primary purposes. First, EFL students will develop and improve all four language skills. Second, they will become more familiar with the content, level, and format of the ECCE test by completing the practice activities, mini-tests, and full test provided in this book.

How to Use This Book

This textbook is designed to be used in an EFL class or for individual study. It may also be used as a single course book or to complement other materials. Classroom teachers using this book will want to plan how to use it based on the number of contact hours they have with students: The book has been designed so that it takes about six to ten hours to complete the exercises in each unit, depending on how much work is done in class or is assigned for homework. We provide classroom activities for 30 to 50 hours and review/ practice tests for an additional 10 to 15 hours. The mini-tests take 40 minutes to administer, and full tests take up to 2½ hours.

The Organization of the Units

There are six units in this book. The content and activities are organized in the following sections: (1) Topic Discussion Activities, (2) Reading, (3) Language, (4) Writing, (5) Listening, and (6) Speaking. While this order does not reflect the order of the activities on the ECCE test itself, organizing the sections in this way makes the units more appropriate for pedagogical purposes in terms of making meaningful associations to learn a language; relating new content and language to what is already known about the topic; and gradually building on previously learned aspects of the language to improve linguistic competence. The sequence proposed in this text helps to make those meaningful connections, and each section will prove a useful aid to subsequent sections.

- The **Topic Discussion Activities** introduce the central theme of the unit. Other activities expand on related themes. These activities also help learners to activate their previous knowledge of the theme and introduce language in context. The vocabulary presented in this section may be useful when elaborating on the topic, even when not all expressions or terms may be tested in exams like the ECCE.

• The **Reading** section presents different genres of reading passages followed by comprehension and language-related activities. Reading passages vary from unit to unit, providing practice with the three main kinds of texts used in the ECCE: short passages, ads (skim/scan), and extended reading passages.

• The **Language Practice** section continues with a variety of ECCE-level grammar and vocabulary activities. The structures and vocabulary included in this section reflect those that will present some difficulty for learners at this level. The practice in this section does not cover all the possible structures or vocabulary that can appear on the ECCE, as no single textbook would ensure that an EFL learner reaches this high level of competence in the language.

• The **Writing** section provides a prompt in the format of the ECCE. We are confident that the work on the previous sections will have provided students with enough information to be able to write on the topic. We recommend that this writing practice is done under the same conditions as with the ECCE—allow only 30 minutes to respond to the prompt writing a 150- to 175-word letter or essay. Afterward, we recommended students become familiar with the writing rubrics used to rate this section of the test. The rubrics are published and updated on the ELI's website: *www.lsa.umich.edu/eli/*.

• The **Listening** section provides practice with the two formats of the ECCE listening tasks. In Part I, examinees listen to short conversations and then are asked about what they heard. Three picture options are presented for response to each question. In Part II, they hear segments of a radio interview and are asked questions about it.

• The **Speaking** section of the test reflects the speaking portion of the ECCE. Since the ECCE speaking tests are conducted by trained examiners, it is not possible to propose the same type of activities in a textbook intended for classroom use. Instead, we have included similar activities that require students to make the same kind of decisions that they would make as part of the Speaking Test. The activities in this text are proposed for pairs of students, and not for an examiner and an exam candidate. The activities provide practice with Tasks 2 and 3 of the ECCE Speaking Test. However, at the end of the Full Test, a speaking prompt is given to students with the Examiner part on the next page. The Examiner reads the prompt in the actual test setting. Teachers who wish to know more about the Examiner's prompts can visit *www.lsa.umich.edu/eli/testing/*.

• **The Mini-Tests** appear after Units 2 and 4. These are abridged versions of ECCE practice tests that allow practice during normal classroom hours. The mini-tests include

10 listening items, 10 grammar items, 10 vocabulary items, and 10 reading items (combining two different types of reading passages). We recommend that, as students become familiar with the multiple-choice format, these tests be timed, allowing no more than 40 minutes to reflect the expectations of the ECCE.

• The **Practice Test** is a full-length test that provides more actual practice with the content, format, and timing of the test. Again, when possible, it should be administered following the same time constraints of the real ECCE. Note that to keep the audio limited to one CD, we have shortened the pauses between items in the listening section by a few seconds. Teachers can add additional time for students by pressing the pause button on the CD player.

We hope to have made preparing for the ECCE a stimulating and engaging endeavor.

—Fernando Fleurquin, John W. McLaughlin, and Amy D. Yamashiro

Ann Arbor, MI, 2006

Language Features Reviewed in Volume 1			
Unit	Topic	Language Forms	Text Types
1	Health and happiness	synonyms/antonyms; active/passive verb forms; subjunctive; contrast markers	scientific health reports
2	Stress and exercise	verb tenses	vacation brochures; radio interview
3	Eating healthy	synonyms/antonyms; noun/adjective forms; adjectival clauses; passive form	news report; short conversations
4	Cooking or eating out	word classifications; comparative sentences	advertisements; brochures; scientific health study; radio interview
5	Children and money	conditional sentences; adverbial phrases	radio interview
6	Friends and family	word categories; transitions; prepositions; phrasal verbs	story; news report; radio interview

Acknowledgments

We would like to thank our colleagues at the ELI-UM with special mention to Diane Larsen-Freeman, Barbara Dobson, and Mary Spaan for their encouraging words and feedback and to the great staff at the UM Press and in particular to our editor, Kelly Sippell, who guided us through the development process from inception to production. We would also like to thank the teachers and students from ELI-UM Test Centers from all over the world who inspired us to write this text. Fernando would like to thank Beatriz Greco, who worked with him on the administration of the ECCE for many years, and who was one of the first to encourage him to write a test-preparation book like this. Most important, Fernando would like to thank his lovely wife Fabiana and his two wonderful sons, Guillermo and Bruno, for their unconditional support, understanding, and love. After spending countless nights and weekends writing and editing sections of this book, John and Amy both greatly appreciate the patience and understanding granted by their adorable toddler, Liam, and their two cats, Ginger and Oscar.

Thanks to the following individuals for voice talent on the accompanying audio: Giles Brown, Amy Fuller, Pat Grimes, Badria Jazairi, Karen Pitton, and Jacob Richardson. Thanks to Kerri Kijewski for additional photos used in the book.

Thanks to Juniper Images for photos and clip art.

Thanks to the English Language Institute for ECCE instruction wording on mini-tests and full test/practice test.

Good Vibes

Topic Discussion Activities

1. Happiness Boosters

Small Group Discussion

From the following list, which type of activity would you recommend to change a friend's sad mood?

☐ watching an old movie

☐ listening to your favorite song

☐ talking to a friend

☐ watching TV

☐ talking to someone in your family

☐ writing about your feelings in a diary or journal

☐ going shopping

☐ reading a book

☐ playing a sport

☐ going out for a walk by yourself

Supporting Your Opinion

Why would you recommend some of these activities to your friend? Why wouldn't you recommend the other activities?

2. Useful Expressions

Do you know these words and phrases? Use them to describe personal experiences.

Feeling	Verbs	Expressions
down/blue/sad upset/angry shocked/stunned/devastated	to cheer someone up to make someone happy to make someone feel better to lessen/ease one's sorrow or pain	in a good/bad mood down in the dumps under the weather not feeling myself lately

ECCE Reading Practice

3. What Do You Think?

In small groups, discuss the following questions.

Many people say that laughter is the best medicine. What do you think?
Can laughter actually cure a disease or solve any problem? Why? Why not?

4. Brainstorming

Complete the chart with different effects you think laughter has on people.

Effects of Laughter

5. Skimming

Read the first paragraph of the Reading Passage. Which effects of laughter are mentioned? Are they positive or negative?

Effects of Laughter

Discuss how your predictions in Exercise 4 compare with what you wrote here in Exercise 5?

6. Missing Phrases

Find the best place for these phrases in the reading as indicated by the numbered blank.

a. ____ resort to unhealthy activities
b. ____ are held in hospitals
c. ____ may actually help me
d. ____ find other people

Reading Passage

Read the passage, and then answer the questions on pages 5 and 6 according to the information given in the passage.

(1) Hearty laughter can change one's mood in an instant. It can erase fear, anger, worry, and sadness. Moreover, research has shown that laughter exercises the heart, lungs, and abdominal muscles. It boosts the immune system and even increases blood flow to the brain. Laughter has also been found to increase alertness, creativity, and memory, while increasing tolerance to pain and lowering blood pressure. However, laughter has often been considered to be the opposite of paying attention or working in schools or business settings.

(2) Recently in the United States, laughter is being recognized for its health benefits. Because of this, there has been rapid growth in the number of laughter clubs being formed each year. One leader explains, "Pre-school kids laugh more than 400 times a day, while most adults have only about 15 daily laughs. This is a shame because laughing is a great stress reducer that actually changes the chemistry of the brain." Laughter experts recommend taking a humor break rather than _____①_____, such as drinking, smoking, or overeating to release tension.

(3) Certified laughter leaders are finding more consulting work with corporations these days. These consultants reduce stress and increase job satisfaction through humor therapy. In fact, they have found that one of the most common reasons why people leave their jobs is not because of their salary; it is because they are unhappy.

(4) One laughter expert explained how laughter helped her: "Although

I couldn't change what happened in my life, I realized I could change my attitude. I discovered that laughter is a physical activity that _____②_____ find and experience inner peace, happiness, and love."

(5) To have more opportunities to enjoy a good laugh each day, you need to _____③_____ who are bubbling over with infectious giggles. When they laugh, you will too. Luckily, people are now recognizing the growing importance of laughter. One example of this new trend is the 200 plus "laughter clubs" that _____④_____, schools, and businesses.

7. Skimming and Scanning

Quickly skim the reading to find the following information. Some of the topics may not be mentioned. If they are, indicate the paragraph where you found them.

		Mentioned? Yes/No	If so, in which paragraph(s)?
1.	The effects of laughter on the body		
2.	Job satisfaction		
3.	The work of laughter experts		
4.	Where the next laughter club will meet		
5.	A personal anecdote		
6.	Cultural attitudes about laughter		
7.	Differences between children and adults about laughing habits		
8.	Suggestions to laugh more		

8. Checking Comprehension

Read the passage on pages 4 and 5 again. Answer the questions. Underline the text in the passage that contains information to answer these questions. Circle the letter of the best response.

1. According to the article, someone who laughs a lot

   a. has high blood pressure

   b. works out a lot

   c. is stressed

   d. fights infections more effectively

2. According to the reading, what should we learn from pre-schoolers?

    a. to laugh in class

    b. to laugh more often

    c. to be 400 times more creative

    d. to take humor breaks

3. According to the article, what can we infer about humor therapy?

    a. It reduces job satisfaction.

    b. It increases blood pressure.

    c. It increases creativity.

    d. It guarantees a better salary.

4. What is the best title for the article?

    a. Laughter Changes Our Brains

    b. Laugh and Look Younger

    c. Laughter Can Help Pre-Schoolers

    d. Laughter: A Useful Resource

9. Identifying Opinions

Decide whether the statement agrees or disagrees with the author's opinion. Circle *agree* or *disagree*. Then decide whether you agree or disagree. Circle *agree* or *disagree*. Find evidence in the article to support these opinions. Give reasons to support these opinions.

	Author's Opinion	My Opinion
Laughter specialists think that happiness is more important than salary.	Agree/Disagree	Agree/Disagree
We can learn a lot from young children.	Agree/Disagree	Agree/Disagree

ECCE Language Practice

10. Vocabulary: Word Forms

Complete the chart using one or more words you know in each box.

Noun	Adjective	Synonyms	Antonym (adjectives)
fear	fearful	afraid, frightened	fearless
anger			
worry			
sadness			
creativity			

11. Vocabulary: Word Categories

Using these words, create groups of related words according to their meaning. There may be different ways to group them. You can use as many boxes as you want from the chart. Then, give each category a name, and have at least two words in each category. An example is provided.

chuckle	gurgle	shout
cry	holler	smile
frown	laugh	wail
giggle	scream	weep
grin	screech	yell

Verbs that May Express Happiness	Category _____	Category _____	Category _____	Category _____
smile giggle				

12. Grammar: Placement of Adverbs in Active and Passive Verb Forms

Use the words in parentheses to complete the sentences. Use the verbs in the correct tense. An example has been done for you.

Example:

Several studies _have repeatedly shown_ (repeatedly/show) that people who laugh more often live longer and are more satisfied with their lives.

1. The validity of the results of such studies _____ (question/recently).

2. An experiment involving teenagers and auto industry workers _____ (conduct/nowadays) in Central America to show the relationship between literacy levels and happiness.

3. Researchers in Ottawa _____ (find/actually) that laughter increased tolerance and reduced anxiety.

4. The work of laughter specialists _____ (recognize/not/publicly) before Dr. Mothe published the results he obtained with multi-national companies just a few years ago.

5. Unhappiness at work _____ (consider/now) the most important reason why companies are requesting psychological counseling for their staff.

13. Sentence Completion

Complete the sentences with information about yourself. Then use them as conversation starters to talk to your partner.

1. I've been recently notified that _____
    _____.

2. A friend of mine was caught _____
    _____.

3. To be happy, it is essential that _____
    _____.

4. In spite of many obstacles, _____
    _____.

5. My family has always recommended that _____
    _____.

ECCE Writing Practice

THE ANN ARBOR TIMES

Happiness: past and future. Some people feel happy when they can have the latest technological gadgets, change their car every year, or move to a larger house. On the other hand, some people feel happy when they can help others; they do not think about their own material possessions. Different people do different things to look for happiness. What does happiness mean to you? *The Ann Arbor Times* wants to know your opinion about how happiness has changed over the years.

14. Writing Exercises

Choose one of the task options.

A. Letter to the Editor

Write a letter to the editor of *The Ann Arbor Times*. Describe first what you think made people happy in the past (e.g., during the time of your parent or grandparents), and then what you think will make people happy in the future. Explain your opinion about the best way to achieve happiness.

B. Essay

Happiness has different meanings to different people. Some say that we can only expect to live "happy moments" in our lives, and that real happiness is impossible to achieve. Others experience moments of happiness just by being in contact with nature, attending a concert, or working on a task they enjoy. What is your definition of happiness? How can happiness be cultivated in society?

ECCE Listening Practice

15. Listening: Short Conversations

After each conversation, a question is asked about what was heard. The possible answers to the question are shown as pictures. Circle the correct answer for each question. Remember that each conversation is heard only once. Conversations are not repeated on the test.

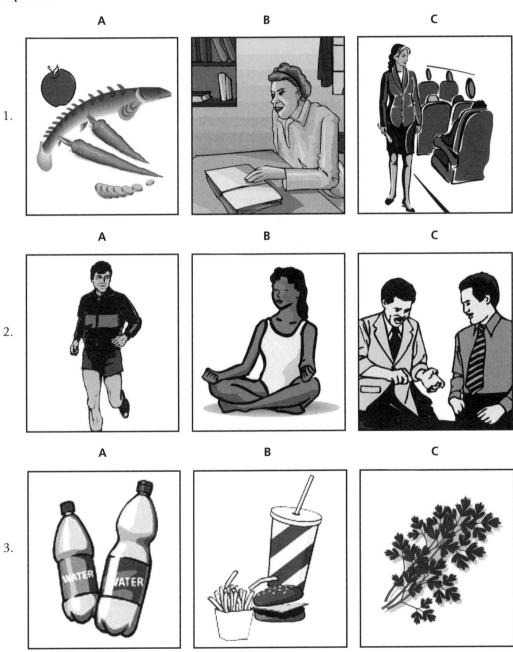

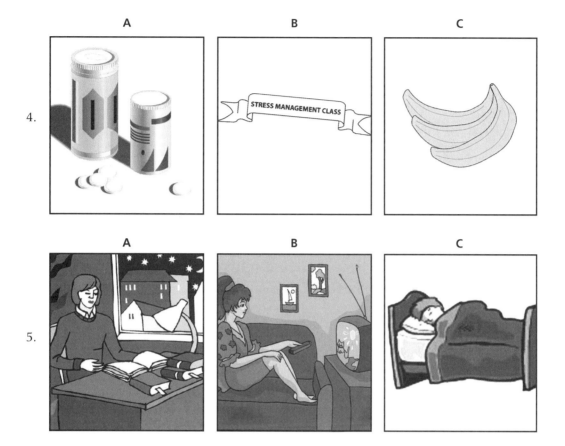

ECCE Speaking Practice

16. Offering Advice

Work in pairs. One of you will look at the information in Box A, and the other one will look at the information in Box B (on page 153). A will ask B questions to find out more about the problem. Then A needs to offer B some advice.

What advice can you offer? Why did you choose that option? Why didn't you choose the other one? *Make sure you use some of the information that B mentioned in your answer.*

A. Your friend has a problem. Ask questions to find out what the problem is and offer your advice.

Look at the pictures and ask:
- Who is this person?
- What is the problem?
- What are the possible solutions?
- What are the advantages and disadvantages of each solution?

17. Elaboration Questions

With a partner, ask each other these questions. Try to spend at least two minutes responding to each question. Encourage each other to develop the topic. Pay attention to the level of detail when elaborating.

1. In what ways can people find happiness by spending time on the Internet?

2. What kind of friendship can you develop with someone you haven't met in person?

3. In what ways can chat rooms be dangerous?

4. In what ways can a person be happy without having a social life and friends who care about him or her?

Stress and Fitness

Topic Discussion Activities

1. Exercising and Health

In small groups, ask and answer the following questions.

1. How much exercise do you get on a daily or weekly basis? How much exercise do you think you should be getting?

2. What is the most unusual sport you've seen? What sports have you played that were unusual for you? What kind of physical activity did you practice for the longest time?

3. How often do you see your doctor? Your dentist?

2. Useful Expressions

Do you know these words? Can you use them to describe personal experiences?

Types of Physical Activity	Words to Describe Sports	Sports
aerobics, jogging, weights, weightlifting, sports, track and field, hiking, cycling, work out, stretch, sit-ups, push-ups, yoga, walking, stretching	indoor, outdoor, aggressive, energetic, tiring, tired, warm-up, exhausting, exhausted, relaxing, invigorating, exhilarating, exciting, tiresome, team and individual sports, spectator	hockey, volleyball, lacrosse, football, soccer, basketball, tennis, racquetball, sand boarding, surfing, snowboarding, jogging, bowling, golf, badminton, polo, swimming, ice-skating

3. Recommendations

Work in groups of three. Ask your classmates no more than five questions, and recommend one kind of physical activity for the other two members of your group. Explain why you think this activity would be good for your group members.

Sample questions: Do you like water sports?
Do you like playing indoor or outdoor sports?
Do you like team or individual sports?

Recommendation: I suggest that you try water polo because . . .
I'd recommend that you try . . .
Why don't you try . . .
I'd encourage you to . . .

4. Reading Brochures

What type of information do you think might appear in brochures about places people go on vacation? Check the pieces of information that you would expect to find in different brochures.

☐ accessibility for persons with disabilities
☐ advantages of the particular place
☐ complaints
☐ costs
☐ disadvantages of the particular place
☐ indoor activities available
☐ maps of the area
☐ names and pictures of staff members
☐ name of the owner(s)

☐ address / specific location
☐ crime rates in the area
☐ directions to the area / place
☐ floor plans
☐ outdoor activities available
☐ name of the place
☐ comments by satisfied customers
☐ working hours

5. Analyzing Options

Work in groups of three. Consider these three vacation spots. You and your friends are thinking about going camping, but you haven't decided where to go yet. Make a list of the advantages and disadvantages of each of the three places. Then decide the one that all of you would like to go to.

Advantages	Advantages	Advantages
Disadvantages	**Disadvantages**	**Disadvantages**

6. Making Predictions

Before reading information from a brochure about a place called Great Lakes Spa, answer these questions.

1. Who do you think this place might appeal to? _____

   _____

2. What activities do you think you may be able to do there? _____

   _____

3. What information you received during Activity 1C may be important for you to decide whether to go there or not? _____

   _____

ECCE Reading Practice

Reading Passage 1

This practice reading has a series of related passages such as those found in public information brochures or magazines. Read the questions on pages 18 and 19, and scan through the text to find the answers.

Great Lakes Spa

Great Lakes Spa is a health and fitness retreat in a stress-free, country setting only 90 miles north of Detroit, Michigan. This spacious 32-acre estate is located on a private lake surrounded by beautiful woods and miles of gently rolling hills. In this peaceful environment, you'll learn how to take good care of yourself so you can feel better, look better, and live better. You'll enjoy a fabulous range of spa and fitness activities in a supportive atmosphere with matchless service.

Individualized Wellness Program

Wellness experts work with you to set realistic goals, develop a personalized working plan, and get you started with a spa program designed to achieve your optimal health. Programs are offered for small groups of up to 32 guests who share a common health objective. You have the opportunity to learn, experience, and utilize the most accurate, available scientific information regarding fitness, nutrition, and stress management. You can begin to make desirable changes in your lifestyle all in a fun-filled, relaxing, environment, supervised by a trained professional staff.

Nutritional Programs

You will learn the basics of healthy eating, balanced diets, optimum nutrition, healthy cooking techniques, and weight-loss management. You will enjoy tempting and satisfying cuisine that includes grilled salmon served over spinach-mushroom ravioli in a broth with ginger, garlic, orange zest, snow peas, and red peppers; or a fresh berries crepe drizzled with vanilla sauce and almonds. *You will not feel deprived.*

Challenge Yourself

Have you ever climbed a rock wall or walked across a rope bridge? These and other activities are all part of the Great Lakes Challenge, a health and fitness program that allows you to experience personal challenge first hand. These activities encourage you to develop yourself both as an individual and as a team member.

Activities

GREAT LAKES CHALLENGE	STRETCH CLASSES	TAI CHI AND QI GONG
A program designed to help you reach new levels of achievement and self-confidence through safe and challenging team activities.	Designed to improve flexibility through basic stretching and a range of movements to release stress through relaxation techniques.	Ancient Chinese exercises that combine meditation and movement. Utilize body, mind, and breathing to develop coordination and awareness to reduce stress.
HEALTH WALK	WATER BIKES	WATER AEROBICS
Choose your own distance and pace in the beautiful countryside surrounding the spa.	Alone or with a friend, paddle your way to fitness around our lovely lake. The safest way to lose some pounds in a few days.	Exercise in the water! This workout session challenges those who have reached an advanced fitness level.
INTERVAL TRAINING	WEIGHT TRAINING	YOGA
Fat burning and muscle building all in one, it combines aerobic moves with muscle conditioning.	Learn to use free weights to develop strength and shape muscles with the proper techniques.	Stretch and energize the body, calm and focus the mind, uplift and nourish the spirit. Learn breathing, relaxation and bodywork techniques.

7. Checking Comprehension

Read the passage on page 17. Answer the questions. Underline the text in the passage that contains information to answer the questions. Circle the letter of the best response.

1. What might you see if you visit the spa?

   a. sand dunes and ocean beaches

   b. hills and trees

   c. Detroit, MI

   d. wild animals in their natural habitat

2. What is highlighted as a key feature of the Great Lakes Spa?

   a. personalized health care attention

   b. self-defense lessons

   c. cooking classes

   d. the active night life

3. Great Lakes Spa nutritional programs teach you how to

   a. prepare a balanced diet based on vegetables

   b. cook ravioli and salmon

   c. lose weight fast

   d. eat better to improve your health

4. A friend of yours has decided to go to the Great Lakes Spa. He is very stressed and has not done any physical activity in years. According to the ads, which activity would be more appropriate for your friend to start with?

   a. interval training

   b. water aerobics

   c. tai chi and qi gong

   d. Great Lakes challenge

5. If you went along with your friend to the spa, which of the following activities could you do together?

   a. water aerobics

   b. Great Lakes challenge

   c. tai chi and qi gong

   d. health walk

6. Which of these activities would be recommended for losing weight?

   a. weight training and stretch classes

   b. water bikes and yoga

   c. interval training and water aerobics

   d. water bikes and interval training

Reading Passage 2

Read the passage, and then answer the questions on pages 20 and 21 according to the information given in the passage.

Migraines are terrible headaches that tend to produce nausea and sensitivity to light and smells in the people who suffer from them. These headaches may last from a few hours to a few days. Some people try prescription medications, yoga, meditation, and massage, but they still may not get any relief from the suffering. Migraines often result from an inadequate supply of blood to the brain. Some researchers are investigating the use of nutritional supplements such as niacin (vitamin B_3) and magnesium. Niacin has been found to promote healthy blood flow that may actually prevent the onset of migraine headaches. Magnesium keeps facial muscles relaxed to prevent contractions that cause migraines and tension headaches. In one study, people who took a daily dose of magnesium reported 42 percent fewer headaches. Another approach has been to design a mouth guard that prevents the wearer from grinding teeth and clenching the jaw during sleep. Experts believe that this nighttime facial tension strains the nerves and muscles in the temples and may account for up to 80 percent of all migraines. In clinical trials, some people got relief the next day, and 82 percent of users experienced 77 percent less pain within eight weeks. Research indicates that migraine sufferers contract their jaw muscles about 14 times more intensely than people who do not get them. One former migraine sufferer said, "It's been four years since I've had a migraine. I'd never have guessed that a little piece of plastic would bring me such relief."

8. Checking Comprehension

Read the passage on pages 19 and 20 again. Answer the questions. Underline the text in the passage that contains information to answer the questions. Circle the letter of the best response.

1. According to the passage, why are researchers interested in studying migraines?

    a. to find out how often they occur

    b. to find more effective ways to prevent and cure them

    c. to try prescription medications for new patients

    d. to understand how patients feel about the different symptoms

2. What do headache experts say causes most migraines?

    a. an inadequate supply of blood to the brain

    b. teeth grinding and jaw clenching during sleep

    c. a lack of the nutritional supplement magnesium

    d. too much time spent meditating or doing yoga

3. What does niacin do?

    a. Facial tension is reduced with this vitamin.

    b. It helps to relax facial muscles during massage.

    c. A daily dose reduces migraines by about 42 percent.

    d. It promotes healthy blood flow.

4. What benefit does magnesium offer?

   a. It prevents facial tension.

   b. It offers nighttime relief from migraines.

   c. It helps prescription medications work better.

   d. It encourages blood flow to the brain.

5. According to the passage, how does the mouth guard work?

   a. It keeps people from grinding their teeth.

   b. It helps people contract their jaws more intensely.

   c. It strains the nerves and muscles in the face.

   d. It promotes blood flow to the brain.

6. How effective is the mouth guard?

   a. It's effective for about four years.

   b. In eight weeks, more than 80 percent of users experience some pain relief.

   c. About 77 percent of pain is gone overnight.

   d. Migraine sufferers have14 times less pain than before.

ECCE Language Practice

9. Vocabulary

Fill in the Blank

Use one of the following words to complete the sentences. If it is a verb, be sure to put it in the correct form. Answers are used only once.

achieve	nourish	relieve
achievement	optimal	retreat
attribute	peak	spacious
deprive	range	supportive
desirable	reach	surroundings

1. I was very fortunate to have such a _____ algebra teacher. She has given me extra assignments to make sure I could catch up with the classes I missed.

2. Last week my back was really stiff from working on the computer for too long. Fortunately, the muscle tension was _____ after I had a massage.

3. Our math teacher received a special award in recognition of his students' impressive _____ in the XII Math Olympics.

4. The two puppies had been left alone, _____ of water and food for more than three days. If we hadn't found them, they would have died.

5. After training for more than six months, the athletes are in _____ condition to compete. They can't get any better than this.

6. We are planning a _____ for all of the school staff to build a better team spirit.

7. What I like about the club I just joined is the wide _____ of people you can meet there.

8. After working out for more than two months, I was able to _____ the expected performance level I wanted.

9. Part of the success of the spa is due to its peaceful and beautiful _____. One feels better just by looking out the window.

10. The most exciting part of the climbing trip was when we got to the _____ of the mountain. We were exhausted, but we were thrilled when we got there.

Make Your Own Sentences

Write sentences using the five words on page 22 that were not used in the Fill-in-the-Blank activity.

1. _____

_____.

2. _____

_____.

3. _____

_____.

4. _____

_____.

5. _____

_____.

10. Grammar: Expressing Contrast

Fill in the blanks with one of these words: *however, although, but, though, in spite of.* Some blanks may have more than one possible answer. The first one has been done for you.

1. Pre-school children laugh freely whenever they want; _____*however*_____, adults tend to hide their emotions and don't laugh as often.

2. _____ the effects of laughter are better known every day, many CEOs still don't trust laughter therapy to improve their employees' productivity and satisfaction.

3. _____ the fitness plan we implemented at our company during the last two years, our employees don't feel they have reached their best physical condition.

4. The lacrosse team captain is an excellent player. He is not a good example to follow when we lose, _____, because of his behavior.

5. The coach gave us excellent suggestions to improve our attack strategies on the field, _____ we didn't practice how to defend our area.

6. _____ eating a balanced diet is part of feeling healthy, one also needs to nurture the mind and the spirit to be a healthy person.

7. Our teacher thinks he can change the mood of the class by giving us an extra break, _____ we don't feel like having fun today.

8. There is ample evidence of the effects of laughter on our lives. _____, I still don't know how to make a boring and negative person like my brother laugh once in a while.

11. Grammar: Subjunctive Forms

Read the quotes from different people. Then, using the introductory expressions provided, write a sentence expressing the main idea from the quote. An example has been provided.

Example:

Angry player: "Don't be so demanding with our schedules, or we'll have to quit this team. We come here to play for fun, not to work."

The players demanded that <u>the coach not be so demanding with their weekly schedules</u>.

1. Jim's fiancée: "Honey, what if my mom joins us for the second week of our honeymoon next month?"

   His fiancée suggested that her mother _____

   _____

2. *Doctor:* "Billy will have monthly medical checkups. That will tell us how he is doing with his allergy."

   It is essential that _____

3. *Branch manager:* "Why don't we start a fitness program during our lunch hour? We could invite all employees to bring healthier food and to get together for an exercise class."

   The branch manager suggested that _____

4. *Co-worker:* "Sally should go out and meet more people. I don't think I've heard her talk about having a date during the last two years."

   Sally's co-worker recommended that she _____

   _____

5. *Fitness teacher:* "One of you will participate in the next track and field competition. So we'll have to practice twice as often during the next two weeks."

   Our fitness teacher proposed that _____

ECCE Writing Practice

THE ANN ARBOR TIMES

The perfect stress reliever. The city of Ann Arbor will host a conference on stress management. Individuals of all ages are being selected for demonstrations of different stress-reducing techniques and treatments, including yoga, tai chi, Pilates, and meditation. Selected patients will get one month of free treatment. Send your nominations to the Editor.

---

12. Writing Exercises

Choose one of the task options.

A. *Letter to the Editor*

Write a letter to the editor of *The Ann Arbor Times*. Think of one person who could benefit from stress treatment for free. Explain what has led the person to be so stressed, and why you think he or she should be part of this free program.

B. *Essay*

Stress is a very common problem in society today. What can people do to make their lives less stressful? What kind of people live a stress-free life? Give specific examples.

ECCE Listening Practice

13. Listening: Short Conversations

After each conversation, a question is asked about what was heard. The possible answers to the question are shown as pictures. Circle the correct answer for each question. Remember that each conversation is heard only once. Conversations are not repeated.

ECCE Speaking Practice

14. Offering Advice

Work in pairs. One of you will look at the information in Box A, and the other one will look at the information in Box B (on page 153). A will ask B questions to find out more about the problem. Then A needs to offer B some advice.

What advice can you offer? Why did you choose that option? Why didn't you choose the other one? *Make sure you use some of the information that B mentioned in your answer.*

A. Your friend has a problem. Ask questions to find out what the problem is and offer your advice.

Look at the pictures and ask:
- Who is this person?
- What is the problem?
- What are the possible solutions?
- What are the advantages and disadvantages of each solution?

15. Elaboration Questions

With a partner, ask each other these questions. Try to spend at least three minutes responding to each question. Encourage each other to develop the topic. Pay attention to the level of detail when elaborating.

1. How many people do you know with this problem? How does being overweight affect them?

2. What eating habits were you taught when you were young?

3. Are there any eating habits that children and teenagers have today that should change?

4. How important do you think eating is in your culture? Is this different from other cultures?

Mini-Test 1

Listening: Radio Interview

Imagine you are listening to the radio. You are going to hear someone from a radio station interviewing one or more people at a special event. You will hear the interview in several parts. After each part, you will hear some questions. There are three answer choices for each question. You should select, from the three answer choices, the best answer to the question. If you want to, you may take notes as you listen.

Remember, after each section of the interview, you will hear some questions. On the test, the sections are separated by double lines. On the test, you will have 12 seconds to mark your answer by circling the letter of the best response.

Segment 1

Notes about Segment 1:

1. a. community fair

   b. medical school

   c. county hospital

2. a. Kelly Fountain

   b. an expert on health

   c. the event organizer

3. a. to separate health-care myths from reality

   b. to help people understand how the body works

   c. to have more people become health-care professionals

Segment 2   *Notes about Segment 2:*

4. a. balance requires neural
        orientation

    b. it's a sign of brain health

    c. it helps to develop balance

5. a. standing with eyes closed for
        more than 45 seconds

    b. standing on one leg for more
        than 20 seconds

    c. working out with free weights
        instead of a machine

6. a. the brain is engaged to
        maintain balance

    b. neural pathways stimulate
        body orientation

    c. the body is challenged to
        orient neural pathways

7. a. they require the body to
        maintain balance

    b. they cause neural activity to be
        more active

    c. the weights are attached to the
        machine

Segment 3

8. a. targeting exercise to a specific area

    b. doing hundreds of sit-ups every day

    c. reducing belly fat by toning the abdomen

9. a. Muscle must be built in particular areas before others.

    b. The trouble spot must be targeted first.

    c. The entire body, not just one part, must be fit.

10. a. build muscle and reduce belly fat

    b. aerobic exercise, resistance work, and diet

    c. tone the problem area through focused exercise

Notes about Segment 3:

Grammar

Choose the word of phrase that best completes the sentence or the conversation.

11. When I have difficulty sleeping, my mother tells me that it _____ to take a warm bath before bedtime.

    a. helps

    b. helping

    c. is helping

    d. helpful

12. "Which group of people do you think get the most benefit from meditation?" "Everyone from young children _____ retirees get something out of doing it."

    a. to

    b. and

    c. until

    d. through

13. "What's the matter with Stuart?"

    "I don't know. He didn't tell me _____ worrying him."

    a. has that been

    b. has been what

    c. what has been

    d. what that has

14. Some people think that it is not necessary _____ to stay home when they catch a cold.

    a. to them

    b. for them

    c. that they

    d. they need

15. If you practice yoga, you will develop

    a. strength and enduring

    b. strength and endurance

    c. strong and enduring

    d. strong and endurance

16. It has been shown in countless research projects that sleep _____ good health.

    a. linked to

    b. is linked to

    c. being linked with

    d. is linking with

17. The government needs _____ the relationship between air quality and health problems.

    a. to take serious

    b. to take seriously

    c. to be taken seriously

    d. being taken serious

18. "Is your blood pressure still very high?"
    "No, it was my brother _____ concerned."

    a. was

    b. he was

    c. who was

    d. he was that

19. When the pressure to meet deadlines is great, many people don't take time _____ breakfast.

    a. to

    b. by

    c. for

    d. with

20. There are many reasons to take vitamins, _____ as having better overall health and well being.

    a. as much

    b. like

    c. so

    d. such

Vocabulary

Choose the word or phrase that best completes the sentence.

21. Some runners prefer to train on _____ roads, because they believe that the uneven ground gives them a better workout.

    a. rough

    b. smooth

    c. right

    d. strict

22. Most people _____ to get more exercise in the summer than in the winter.

    a. direct

    b. perform

    c. tend

    d. serve

23. Last year, Mary started ordering her vitamins on-line and has them _____ every month.

    a. carried

    b. delivered

    c. transported

    d. moved

24. Eating fast food may be _____, but often the choices are not very nutritious.

    a. anxious

    b. punctual

    c. convenient

    d. easygoing

25. Most fitness experts recommend developing a support _____ when starting a new diet or exercise program.

    a. custom

    b. pattern

    c. combination

    d. network

26. Parents and teachers plan to _____ their efforts to raise money for the school.

    a. call

    b. unite

    c. devise

    d. meet

27. When Oscar was a young child his health was very _____, but now he is very active and fit.

    a. delicate

    b. robust

    c. vigorous

    d. ailing

28. Yesterday, Lisa spent 20 minutes _____ her dog around the park before she caught him.

    a. chasing

    b. running

    c. hunting

    d. seeking

29. Doctors disagree as to when it is best to _____ a patient of a serious health problem.

    a. report

    b. reveal

    c. announce

    d. inform

30. There is a new trend for busy professionals to _____ personal trainers.

    a. contract

    b. hire

    c. take

    d. occupy

Reading—Part I

Read the passage, and then answer the questions on page 38 according to the information given in the passage.

A recent study of more than 1,000 women ages 21 to 58 found that those who had a large social support network of friends and relatives were less likely to suffer from the blues overall. "Women who saw themselves as more loved and cared for were well protected against later episodes of major depression," explains health expert Brandon Wellington, a professor of psychiatry at the University of Minnesota. Having social support may help keep a woman's heart healthy as well. According to a study of more than 500 women with an average age of 59, those who had many social contacts—and saw them often—were less likely to die of heart disease than those who spent more time alone. Compared with more solitary women, they were also 8 percent less likely to have high blood pressure. Socially active women were 11 percent less likely to have diabetes and 10 percent less likely to smoke. Although these studies focused on women, medical experts believe that men benefit from supportive networks as well. It's important for both genders to refrain from do-it-yourself or "retail" therapy. Rather than seeing a movie alone, it's better to call or visit a friend. It's good for both the spirit and the heart.

31. What is the main idea of the passage?

    a. the importance of friends to feel good

    b. the dangers of depression

    c. how to have a healthy heart

    d. good spirits lead to good health

32. Which group is more likely to suffer from depression?

    a. younger women

    b. solitary women

    c. women with friends

    d. women who smoke

33. Social contacts directly help women's heart health, because they reduce the risk of women

    a. suffering the blues

    b. dying from heart disease

    c. using "retail" therapy

    d. feeling unloved and alone

34. In the passage, what is meant by the word *retail*?

    a. spending time with friends

    b. shopping for fun

    c. buying pills

    d. spending money

35. According to the passage, what is an additional benefit of having friends?

    a. spending more time alone

    b. reduced odds of diabetes

    c. fewer opportunities to smoke

    d. higher blood pressure

Reading—Part II

Read the questions on page 40 first, and then look in this text for the answers.

Clutter contributes to that over-tired feeling that can crop up even when you stop to take a television break on the couch. Follow these simple organizing tips to reduce stress and relax.

❶ For the coffee table, feng shui experts recommend storing books and magazines in closed boxes under the table to keep your mind clear.

❷ Piles of CDs and DVDs can drive most people crazy. Use small wicker baskets designed for storing them. They look warmer for the living room, and since they are inexpensive each family member can have one for his or her personal collection.

❸ Expand storage under the television by using a low, wide bench with open shelves. Use large wicker bins that work like drawers for storing toys and other articles.

❹  To keep track of the remote controls for the television and other electronic equipment, use an office organizer for standing files.

36. According to the passage, what helps us to relax?

    a. clutter in the house

    b. piles of things

    c. organizing tips

    d. personal collections

37. According to the passage, what do feng shui experts suggest?

    a. taking breaks to watch television

    b. reading magazines and books

    c. keeping the coffee table free of clutter

    d. storing the coffee table in a box

38. What is the usual purpose of an office organizer?

    a. to hold files and supplies

    b. to keep track of remote controls

    c. to prevent overtired feelings

    d. to reduce stress on the couch

39. Why does the passage recommend using wicker baskets?

    a. they contribute to clutter

    b. people like to collect them

    c. they drive people crazy

    d. they make the room feel cozier

40. What is the purpose of this article?

    a. to give useful ideas

    b. to report on a design

    c. to describe a process

    d. to explain feng shui

Eating "Good" Stuff

Topic Discussion Activities

1. Foods and Eating

In small groups, ask and answer the following questions.

1. What is your favorite kind of food?

2. When you eat out, where do you like to go?

3. How often do you go to a fast-food restaurant?

4. What do you hear people say about fast food?

5. What has made these restaurants so popular in the last decade?

2. Find Someone Who . . .

Try to find a different student who answers *yes* for every question, and write the student's name after the items. If you get a *no*, let her or him ask you a question and take turns until you both get an affirmative answer. If that's not possible, after a few tries, think of a short response to a *no*, such as *okay, I see,* or *let's move on.*

> Example:
>
> *Do you know how to cook french fries?*

Find someone who . . .

a. knows how to cook french fries _____

b. knows what country tiramisu is from _____

c. can name three different kinds of salad dressings _____

d. can describe how to prepare an omelet _____

e   has never been on a diet _____

f. doesn't like sushi _____

g. can tell the difference between baking and cooking _____

h. looks at the calories and ingredients before buying food _____

i. has tried snails _____

j. likes different kinds of ethnic foods _____

3. Plan a Party Menu

You and your friends are planning a party. Plan the types of food you want to have for the party. Work in groups and agree on what you want, how much you should buy, and how much each of you will have to pay.

ECCE Reading Practice

4. Predicting

The following terms appear in the Reading on pages 44 and 45. What do you think it will be about?

customers	hospital	philosophical
food choices	obese	royalty
franchise	patients	wellness
heart patients		

5. Fill in the Blank

Read the following passage. When you finish, find the best place for these phrases in the reading passage.

___ a. *including more than 4,800 heart operations*

___ b. *who was in a hurry and*

___ c. *putting their hearts and arteries at grave risk*

___ d. *renowned for its research on heart disease*

Reading Passage

Read the passage, and then answer the questions on pages 45–47.

(1) Anthony Jackson stared at his lunch and agonized about whether his doctor might be disappointed with him. The 59-year-old heart patient had just bought a fried chicken sandwich from the fast-food counter of Utah's most famous hospital, ① _____.

(2) "Many patients have heart problems. When I don't eat in the cafeteria and come here to eat, I cannot resist comfort foods. It's just too tempting," said Jackson, ② _____ didn't want to fight the crowd at the other hospital restaurants and food outlets.

(3) Even so, Jackson agrees with the efforts by the hospital's leading doctors to get some fast-food franchises out of the building. One pizza-maker has already left. But, nine other fast-food franchises remain, including ones that serve hamburgers and deli sandwiches.

(4) At a time when more than two-thirds of American adults are overweight or obese, ③ _____, health officials and physicians are urging people to watch their weight and eat healthier food.

(5) "Serving hamburgers and french fries in the food court of a leading heart treatment center sends the public the wrong message," says one hospital official.

(6) "We are looking to create a trend that raises awareness and connects good nutritional choices with wellness," said Angela Goodman, a hospital spokeswoman. "We are not singling out hamburger and pizza franchises. We're looking at every vendor in the hospital and asking if what's offered on the menu reflects what we are trying to teach our patients about healthy eating."

(7) The patients at Utah Hospital include royalty and leaders of foreign countries, and some of the nation's most prominent heart researchers and surgeons work there. Its heart center treats more than 265,000 patients a year and performs thousands of heart procedures annually, ④ _____.

(8) Nationwide, there does not seem to be much of a trend toward eliminating fast-food companies from hospitals. "We are in about 36 hospitals right now and have been for quite some time," said Thomas Hartman, a senior vice president who oversees the nation's leading hamburger franchise's "balanced lifestyle initiative," which promotes healthy food choices and physical fitness.

(9) Julie Pike, the head of the Western Association of Health Care Administrators, said she is unaware of any other health clinics or treatment centers following Utah Hospital's lead.

(10) "It becomes a philosophical question that has to be answered by the administrators of each hospital," Pike said. "Do we serve healthy foods because we work in a health-care facility, or do we serve what the customers really want to eat? Hospitals all over the country have fast-food options."

(11) It is not uncommon for hospitals to earn money by leasing space to food court companies and restaurants. The hospital would not comment on details of its leases, including how much money it might lose if the fast-food franchises leave. One franchise alone serves 12,000 people annually.

6. Skimming

Skim the article. What information is mentioned about people in the reading?

1. Anthony Jackson: _____

2. Angela Goodman: _____

3. Thomas Hartman: _____

4. Julie Pike: _____

7. Understanding Main Ideas

Read the passage again. Answer the questions. Underline the text in the passage that contains information to answer the questions.

1. Where does this story take place?

2. What is the main problem that is described?

3. What is the "trend" the hospital wants to promote?

4. What is the philosophical question that all hospitals must answer?

8. Checking Comprehension

Read the passage on pages 44 and 45 again. Answer the questions. Underline the text in the passage that contains information to answer these questions. Circle the letter of the best response.

1. Anthony Jackson

   a. works at the hospital

   b. is a patient at the hospital

   c. manages the hospital restaurant

   d. is visiting a patient at the hospital

2. Anthony Jackson

   a. doesn't buy fast food from the hospital restaurant

   b. thinks that there shouldn't be fast-food restaurants in hospitals

   c. is a leader of a foreign country

   d. dislikes fast food

3. According to the passage, the hospital

   a. is implementing changes to promote healthier eating habits

   b. will eliminate all fast-food franchises from the hospital

   c. is setting an example that many other hospitals are following

   d. restaurant serves 12,000 people

4. Thomas Hartman

   a. works for the hospital

   b. works for a fast-food restaurant company

   c. is a physical fitness trainer

   d. regularly visits 36 hospitals

5. According to the passage, more than 265,000 patients

   a. are admitted to the hospital every year

   b. are treated at the heart center each year

   c. are operated on at the heart center

   d. eat at the hamburger and pizza franchises per year

6. According to the passage, if hospitals didn't rent space to fast-food franchises,

    a. patients would not eat

    b. patients would complain

    c. the hospital would save a lot of money

    d. the hospital would lose money

7. The "balanced lifestyle initiative"

    a. proposes to reduce the number of fast-food restaurants in hospitals

    b. is proposed by a hamburger restaurant

    c. is being implemented by the hospital

    d. has been abandoned by 36 hospitals now

8. Which of these would be the best title for this passage?

    a. Hospital Meals Cannot Get Any Worse Now

    b. Learning Philosophy the Hard Way

    c. Hospital Investments Determine the Quality of the Service

    d. Does Fast Food Clash with Hospital Values?

ECCE Language Practice

9. Vocabulary: Synonyms

These words are synonyms for words that appear in the reading. The numbers in parentheses refer to the paragraph in the reading where they appear. Find the synonyms, and write them next to the corresponding word. The first one has been done for you.

a. looked (1)   _____stared_____

b. fat (4)   _____

c. doctor (4)   _____

d. famous (7)   _____

e. building (10)   _____

10. Vocabulary: Word Forms

Complete the chart with the correct word form (noun, related adjective, and its antonym).

Noun	Adjective	Antonym (for adjectives)
health	healthy	unhealthy
	aware	
balance		
	tempting	
	disappointing	

11. Vocabulary: Business Terms

Use one of the words from the list to complete the sentences.

budget	franchise	revenue
dues	lease	royalties
fee	proceeds	vendors

1. To open a _____ in this area, you have to contact our main office in Seattle.

2. The author of that cook book receives _____ of more than $50,000 per year.

3. The registration _____ to become a member of this cooking club is $25.

4. Our hotel has very high standards for hiring new _____.

5. The _____ from the fundraising campaign were donated to the Children's Hospital.

6. The Board of Directors was extremely satisfied with the new products that have generated more than $500,000 in _____.

7. Our company is looking for new offices. The _____ we have expires in two months.

8. This will be a difficult year financially. We have to make sure that all our expenses are included in the _____.

12. Grammar: Relative Clauses

Combine the two sentences into one complete sentence using relative pronouns. Watch punctuation. This is a useful practice when making descriptions, giving details, writing summaries, and listening to rapid speech.

1. Julie Pike is unaware of other hospitals following Utah's example. She is the head of the Western Association of Health Care Administrators.

   Julie Pike, who is head of the Western Association of Health Care Administrators, is unaware of other hospitals following Utah's example.

2. The pizza-maker has already left the concession area inside Utah Hospital. The same pizza-maker has opened three franchises in the surrounding area of the hospital.

   _____

   _____

3. Most of the major fast-food chain restaurants in the nation are in the hospital food court. It is located on the fourth floor.

   _____

   _____

4. Authorized vendors submit a monthly report of their activities. They need to meet the quality standards of the hospital to be accepted.

   _____

   _____

5. Some of the most prominent physicians and researchers are employed by Utah Hospital. It is renowned for its research in the area of heart disease.

   _____

   _____

6. Utah Hospital patients really feel at home when they are there and forget they are being treated. Many of its patients come from Latin America, Europe, and Asia.

   _____

   _____

7. Serving unhealthy foods in hospitals is the trend. Many health authorities are seriously concerned about this trend.

_____

_____

8. On the other hand, with these new franchises, hospitals can make a lot of money. This money can be used to support more medical research projects.

_____

_____

13. Grammar: Identifying and Correcting Errors

Identify which sentences are grammatically correct (C) and which ones are incorrect (I). For the incorrect ones, provide the correct form above the incorrect one. There may be more than one error in a sentence.

C	I	
		1. Selling french fries in a hospital do not contribute to improve the patients' health.
		2. The lifestyles who promote healthy food choices are essential to help heart disease patients.
		3. Urged to watch his own weight, Dr. Peterson has started a new diet under the supervision of the head nutritionist.
		4. The new chef recommend that the soup is pre-heated before serving its.
		5. However you may need several unusual spices for this recipe, it may be worth a try.

ECCE Writing Practice

THE ANN ARBOR TIMES

Better meals at school. An initiative has been proposed to improve the quality of snacks offered to children at schools. If this initiative is approved, soda, chips, and candy will not be sold at schools anymore. *The Ann Arbor Times* is requesting readers' opinions on this issue.

14. Writing Exercises

Choose one of these task options.

A. Letter to the Editor

Write a letter to the editor of *The Ann Arbor Times.* Explain whether you agree or disagree with the proposal. Give specific reasons to support your opinion.

B. Essay

Should schools provide the snacks and meals that students want to eat, or should schools respect what health specialists say is good for children?

ECCE Listening Practice

15. Listening: Conversations

After each conversation, a question is asked about what was heard. The possible answers to the question are shown as pictures. Circle the correct answer for each question. Remember that each conversation is heard only once. Conversations are not repeated.

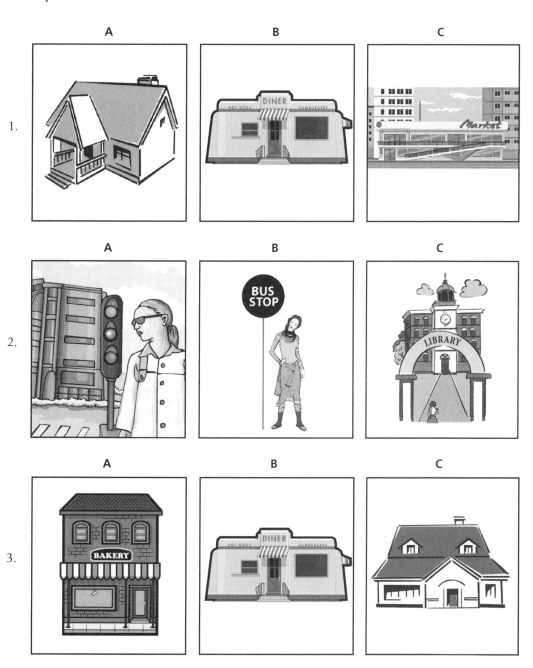

ECCE Speaking Practice

16. Offering Advice

Work in pairs. One of you will look at the information in Box A, and the other one will look at the information in Box B (on page 154). A will ask B questions to find out more about the problem. Then A needs to offer B some advice.

What advice can you offer? Why did you choose that option? Why didn't you choose the other one? *Make sure you use some of the information that B mentioned in your answer.*

A. Your friend has to make a decision. Ask questions to find out what the problem is and offer your advice.

Look at the pictures and ask:
- Who is this person?
- What is the problem?
- What are the possible solutions?
- What are the advantages and disadvantages of each solution?

17. Elaboration Questions

With a partner, ask each other the following questions. Try to spend at least three minutes responding to each question. Encourage each other to develop the topic. Pay attention to the level of detail when elaborating.

1. How healthy are your eating habits?

2. Where can you learn more about eating and cooking healthy meals?

3. What were your favorite meals as a child? What are your favorite meals now?

4. Do you know how to cook? What do you like to cook? What would you like to learn how to cook?

5. There are many kinds of eating problems, such as obesity, bulimia, or anorexia. How much information is available about these problems? Do you think that society contributes to increasing or solving these problems? How?

Eating to Live or Living to Eat?

Topic Discussion Activities

1. Small Group Discussion

In small groups, ask and answer the following questions.

1. Where do you go to buy food?

2. Which do you prefer: to go out to eat or to have a home-cooked meal?

3. Do you or does someone you know follow a special diet?

4. Do you know anyone who lives to eat?

5. Are there any eating habits that you don't like?

2. Creative Uses for Food

Baking soda can be used to remove odors from the refrigerator and for brushing teeth. In small groups, can you think of other ways these food items can be used?

1. salt _____

2. carrots _____

3. rice _____

4. olive oil _____

5. vinegar _____

3. Categories in a Supermarket

Organize the following words in the correct category. An example has been done for you.

beef	chocolate chips	fish	pot holder
butter	chopping board	milk	soda pop
candy	coffee	mixing bowl	tea
can opener	cookies	nuts	wine
cheese	crackers	pork	yogurt
chicken	eggs	potato chips	

Meat	Dairy	Beverages	Snacks	Kitchenware

ECCE Reading Practice

Reading Passage 1

❶ Trader Jack

Affordable Gourmet Foods

Small Store, Friendly Staff

Good Selection of Wines, Cheeses, and Chocolates

Bakery on site for pastries, bread, and desserts

Store Hours:
11 AM–9 PM M–F
10 AM–10 PM SAT
12–6 PM SUN

❷ Saver's Club

Brand-name products for less.

Warehouse store.

No other store will save you more money.
Buy in bulk for great savings.

Members only.

Warehouse Hours:
7 AM–7 PM M–F
9 AM–5 PM SAT
Closed SUN

Rainbow Grocer

We offer the widest and finest selection of international foods and beverages.

If we don't have it, we'll order it direct for you.

Cooking classes every Saturday at 3:00 PM.

Hours:
10 AM–8 PM M–F
11 AM–8 PM SAT
11 AM–6 PM SUN

❹ Green's Food Co-op

Specializing in natural and organic foods.

Great selection of whole-grain breads baked fresh everyday.

Classes on healthy cooking every Tuesday at 7:30 PM.

Membership required.

Hours of Operation:
MWF, 9 AM–6 PM
T & TH, 12–9 PM
SAT & SUN, 10 AM–5 PM

Farmer's Market

We have the best farm-fresh produce in town.

Everything is organic and locally grown.

Come early for the best selection.

Open
Wednesdays and Saturdays from 6:30 AM

4. Scanning for Information
Answer the questions according to the information provided in the ads on page 58. Numbers correspond to ad numbers.

1. If you want to find good food at lower costs and without additional fees, where should you go?

   a. 1

   b. 2

   c. 3

   d. 4

2. If you are making an ethnic dish with special ingredients, which place may have everything you need?

   a. 2

   b. 3

   c. 4

   d. 5

3. Which places require shoppers to become members?

   a. 1 and 2

   b. 1 and 4

   c. 2 and 4

   d. 1, 3, and 5

4. It's 8:00 AM on Saturday, and you want to buy fresh fruit. Where can you go?

   a. 1

   b. 2

   c. 4

   d. 5

5. Which places offer baked goods?

   a. 1 and 3

   b. 1 and 4

   c. 3 and 4

   d. 4 and 5

6. Where can you learn to cook?

    a. 1 and 3

    b. 2 and 4

    c. 3 and 4

    d. only 4

7. Which place(s) sell(s) organic foods?

    a. 1 and 2

    b. 3

    c. 4

    d. 4 and 5

8. You are planning a surprise party and want to get some unusual and special meals. Where would you go for the best selection?

    a. 1

    b. 2

    c. 1 and 4

    d. 3 and 5

9. You are late for a birthday party. You need to get a cake for the party that starts in one hour. Where can you go?

    a. 1

    b. 1 or 3

    c. 5

    d. 2 or 4

10. Which places are open on Sundays?

    a. 1, 2, 3, and 4

    b. 3, 4, and 5

    c. all except 2

    d. all except 2 and 5

11. It's 8:00 on Saturday morning, and you want to get apples from local farms. You don't like foods with pesticides or chemicals. Where can you go?

    a. 1 and 3

    b. 4 and 5

    c. 2, 4, and 5

    d. 5

12. If you have a large family and want to buy some ingredients that will last you for two months or longer, where would you find the best price?

    a. 2 only

    b. 3 and 4

    c. 2 and 5

    d. 1 and 4

5. Matching

Read the following sections from a brochure. From the list, choose the best title for each section. Write the number of the best title above each section.

    a. The Color of Energy

    b. The Secret to Cleaner, Clearer Skin

    c. Improve Your Skin by Drinking Juice

    d. Replace Vitamin Pills with Fruit

    e. Oranges Boost the Immune System

    f. A Sweet Way to Reduce Stress

Reading Passage 2

1. _____

Prized for their ability to fight off infections, oranges are one of nature's richest sources of vitamins. This nutrient helps to prevent damage caused by free radicals and promotes the production of white blood cells that keep the body healthy and strong. Plus, just one orange provides 93 percent of the recommended daily allowance of Vitamin C, making it a tasty way to maintain a healthy immune system.

2. _____

Orange juice gets its tangy flavor from citric acid, a non-irritating anti-bacterial agent that is also highly effective as a skin cleanser. "When the diluted juice is applied to the skin, the mild acid works as an antiseptic to eliminate bacteria that causes acne and blemishes," explains a dermatologist from the University of Norway. "It also acts as a gentle exfoliator, removing dead cells to reveal smoother skin."

3. _____

The sweet scent of oranges instantly begins to work as a stress reliever. According to a recent study at the University of Vienna in Austria, researchers found that when the aroma was pumped into a dentist's waiting room, the patients reported feeling calmer than those who were not exposed to the smell. Experts in aromatherapy say that the scent triggers the release of mood-lifting serotonin in the brain.

4. _____

Orange is a sunny color that restores and refreshes people. "People universally report feeling more mentally and physically alert and energized after being exposed to the color orange," says a color expert from the University of Idaho. In fact, studies show that gazing at this color for mere seconds stimulates the nervous system, increasing heart and breathing rates for a boost of energy.

6. Checking Comprehension

Read the passage on page 62 again. Answer the questions. Underline the text in the passage that contained information to answer these questions. Circle the letter of the best response.

1. Why do oranges have a tangy flavor?

    a. because they eliminate bacteria

    b. because of the citric acid

    c. because of the Vitamin C

    d. because of the juice

2. Where are the researchers who studied the effects of oranges' aroma?

    a. The School of Dentistry

    b. University of Norway

    c. University of Idaho

    d. University of Vienna

3. According to the information in the brochure, our hearts beat faster after

    a. eating an orange

    b. smelling an orange

    c. looking at the color orange for a few seconds

    d. tasting a fresh orange

4. Looking at the orange color for less than one minute

    a. eliminates bacteria

    b. releases the brain

    c. increases our energy level

    d. gives us additional doses of Vitamin C

5. According to the information in the brochure, orange juice can be used to treat acne because

   a. the acid is a good antiseptic

   b. it kills skin cells

   c. it generates white blood cells

   d. it releases serotonin

6. By eating two oranges a day,

   a. we may stay awake at night

   b. we will not feel pain if a dentist is pulling out a tooth

   c. we will have soft and clean skin

   d. we get more than the necessary dose of Vitamin C

7. According to the information in the brochure, serotonin must affect people's

   a. feelings and state of mind

   b. immune system

   c. free radicals

   d. sleep

8. Which of the following effects is not associated with oranges?

   a. fight infections

   b. increase sense of taste

   c. stress relief

   d. faster breathing rate

9. Patients in the study reported by the University of Vienna

   a. showed a positive response after eating oranges

   b. reacted to the orange color of the walls

   c. felt better after smelling the orange aroma in the room

   d. drank and smelled oranges before meeting their dentist

10. What is an exfoliator?

    a. It removes bacteria from the skin.

    b. It generates new skin.

    c. It maintains the immune system.

    d. It removes dead cells.

11. According to the information in the brochure, oranges are good for the skin because of the effects of

    a. Vitamin C

    b. its color

    c. serotonin

    d. citric acid

12. Serotonin

    a. can be found in oranges

    b. can be found in the brain

    c. contributes to fight infections

    d. is used by dentists to put patients to sleep

ECCE Language Practice

7. Vocabulary: Word Categories

Using the words, create groups of related words according to their meaning. There may be different ways to group them. Then, give each category a name, and have at least two words in each category. Examples are given.

bagel	coffee shop	meal
brunch	crispy	restaurant
bun	crunchy	sauce
cafeteria	donut	snack
chewy	dressing	syrup

Places Where You Can Eat			
cafeteria coffee shop			

8. Grammar: Comparative Sentences

Write sentences using the words. Use the adjective in the comparative form. Add any other words you need. Change the form if necessary.

Example:

ice cream, cake, good. For me, ice cream is better than cake.

1. actors, famous, presidents

_____

2. sister, friendly, brother

_____

3. pizza, easy, pasta

_____

4. aunt, drive, carefully, uncle

_____

5. accountant, honest, manager

_____

6. friend, enthusiastic, parents

_____

7. dog, happy, cat

_____

8. fish, quiet, birds

_____

9. Grammar: Verbal Phrases

Choose the best option to complete the sentences.

1. _____ contribute to improve the patients' health.

   a. Selling french fries in a hospital doesn't

   b. Not selling french fries in a hospital

   c. Don't sell french fries in a hospital will

2. _____ the risk of becoming obese, many Americans are being closely monitored by interdisciplinary teams specializing in internal medicine, cardiology, and nutrition.

   a. To run

   b. Running

   c. Run

3. _____ more than 3,000 patients during the last year, Dr. Waterford has become the leading authority in obesity and eating disorders in our hospital.

   a. He sees

   b. Seeing

   c. Having seen

4. _____ to the public's demand, the new hamburgers are not as big and come with a choice of salad or soup.

   a. Responded

   b. Responding

   c. To have responded

5. _____ more than 30 books on nutrition and dieting in less than five years, Kathy Steinfeld can answer any questions about food and eating.

   a. Having to write

   b. Writing

   c. Having written

6. _____ for the summer, many college students start an intense physical training program a few weeks before the end of the school year.

   a. Not to stay in shape

   b. To look in good shape

   c. Looking good

7. _____ Alfredo sauce instead of marinara sauce implies a reduction of 60 percent of the calories of a pasta meal.

   a. Choosing

   b. Choose

   c. Choice

8. We had been warned_____ to Paliotti for dinner. We had to pay a fortune for a very simple meal. We ended up having pizza afterward.

   a. against going

   b. from going

   c. to go

10. Grammar: Verbal Phrases

Complete the sentences using the verb in parentheses in the correct form.

Note that these grammatical forms are more likely to appear in writing or formal speeches.

1. _____ (design) for elementary school children, the book illustrates how the body processes different food elements.

2. _____ (serve) less than 12,000 people annually, this franchise is one of the least successful in the county.

3. _____ (instruct) the vice-president how to take care of critical issues during his absence, the president of the company took a two-month vacation in Cancun.

4. When we were children, we got accustomed to _____ (have) milk with our dinner.

5. It was very embarrassing _____ (not remember) the name of the teacher you met last night at the restaurant.

6. Have you ever considered _____ (become) a chef?

7. It was outrageous. The waiter didn't allow us to leave the restaurant until we consented _____ (leave) him a tip of 25 percent of the bill.

8. It wasn't such a good idea to have the waiter _____ (bring) some more wine after our dinner. We drank too much.

ECCE Writing Practice

THE ANN ARBOR TIMES

Fighting hunger. A large part of the population is considered obese is some countries, including the USA. On the other hand, many children all over the world are homeless and do not have any food to eat. This affects entire countries in Africa, Asia, and Latin America. *The Ann Arbor Times* wants to hear your opinion about a special campaign we can all participate in to raise funds to eradicate hunger from the world.

11. Writing Exercises

Choose one of the task options.

A. Letter to the Editor

Write a letter to the editor of *The Ann Arbor Times*. Describe a campaign that you would propose to fight hunger in the world. Give reasons to support your opinion.

B. Essay

What specific things can we do at a personal or community level to fight hunger? Give specific examples to support your views.

ECCE Listening Practice

12. Before Listening

The following words are taken from the radio interview. What do you think the speakers will be talking about?

frugal   dish   contestant   value   recipe   chef   competition

13. Listening: Radio Interview

Imagine you are listening to the radio. You are going to hear someone from a radio station interviewing one or more people at a special event. You will hear the interview in several parts. After each part, you will hear some questions. There are three answer choices for each question. You should select, from the three answer choices, the best answer to the question. If you want to, you may take notes as you listen.

Remember, after each section of the interview, you will hear some questions. On the test, the sections are separated by double lines. On the test, you will have 12 seconds to mark your answer by circling the letter of the best response.

Segment 1

1. a. a chef
   b. a contestant
   c. a reporter

2. a. a chef
   b. a contestant
   c. a reporter

3. a. a cooking contest
   b. an eating competition
   c. a shopping contest

4. a. Los Angeles
   b. Seattle
   c. Denver

Notes about Segment 1:

Segment 1

5. a. People in North America travel a lot.

   b. They create a dish while spending little money.

   c. They participate in a weekly cooking show.

Notes about Segment 1 (cont.):

Segment 2

6. a. He wanted to use woks.

   b. He got an idea from another show.

   c. He wanted to have a bigger budget.

7. a. It is not part of the food budget.

   b. It must be cooked in an iron wok.

   c. It is used in Japanese cooking.

8. a. just one

   b. three plus dessert

   c. as many as possible

Notes about Segment 2:

ECCE Speaking Practice

14. Offering Advice

Work in pairs. One of you will look at the information in Box A, and the other one will look at the information in Box B (on page 154). A will ask B questions to find out more about the problem. Then A needs to offer some advice.

What advice can you offer? Why did you choose that option? Why didn't you choose the other one? *Make sure you use some of the information that B mentioned in your answer.*

A. Your friend has to make a decision. Ask questions to find out what the problem is and offer your advice.

Look at the pictures and ask:
- Who is this person?
- What is the problem?
- What are the possible solutions?
- What are the advantages and disadvantages of each solution?

15. Elaboration Questions

With a partner, ask each other these questions. Try to spend at least two minutes responding to each question. Encourage each other to develop the topic. Pay attention to the level of detail when elaborating.

1. Where would you like to go on an ideal date?

2. Do you prefer to eat at home or to eat out? Why?

3. How important is honesty in a relationship? Do you know anyone who had problems because of not being honest?

4. How can you tell if a person is lying?

Mini-Test 2

Listening: Short Conversations

This is a test of your ability to understand spoken English. You will hear short conversations. After you hear each conversation, you will be asked a question about what you heard. The answer choices in your test booklet are shown as pictures. Mark your answer by circling the letter of the best response.

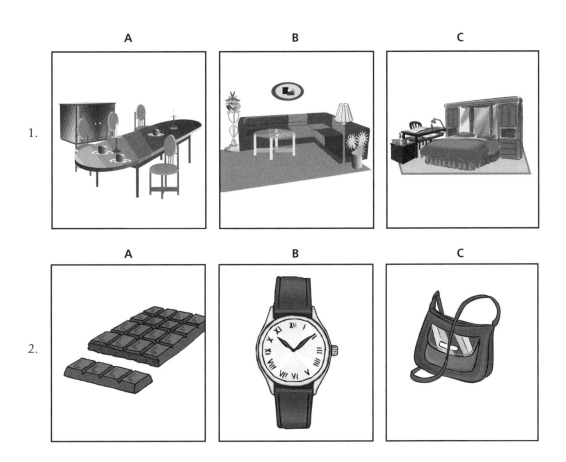

Listening: Radio Interview

Imagine you are listening to the radio. You are going to hear someone from a radio station interviewing one or more people at a special event. You will hear the interview in several parts. After each part, you will hear some questions. There are three answer choices for each question. You should select, from the three answer choices, the best answer to the question. If you want to, you may take notes as you listen.

Remember, after each section of the interview, you will hear some questions. On the test, the sections are separated by double lines. On the test, you will have 12 seconds to mark your answer by circling the letter of the best response.

Segment 1

6. a. He's a news reporter.

    b. He's the event organizer.

    c. He's a financial planner.

7. a. prepare a family budget

    b. look at habits and goals

    c. decrease stress and plan

8. a. hire a financial advisor

    b. start planning by themselves

    c. he gave no suggestion

Notes about Segment 1:

Segment 2

9. a. controlling spending

    b. going into debt

    c. losing their chances

10. a. having too many hobbies

    b. spending a lot of money on toys

    c. buying things that are rarely used

Notes about Segment 2:

Grammar

Choose the word or phrase that best completes the sentence or conversation.

11. "Are we going to Mom's house for dinner on Sunday?"

    "This weekend is _____ the question. I must study for the big exam."

    a. not

    b. without

    c. out of

    d. outside

12. Jeff's wife _____ with his plan to save money for retirement.

    a. to agree

    b. having agreed

    c. agreeing

    d. agreed

13. When Theresa took her entire family out to dinner, the large meal _____ more than she had expected.

    a. added with

    b. added in to

    c. added together

    d. added up to

14. People who do not learn to live within a budget often _____ afford to buy a house.

    a. aren't

    b. can't

    c. don't

    d. won't

15. With college expenses being so high, many students _____ at home after they graduate.

    a. are to live still

    b. are still living

    c. living still

    d. still living

16. At his current job, Brian does not make _____ his family.

    a. enough money to support

    b. money enough to support

    c. enough support money to

    d. to support enough money

17. In my family, I was _____ one to graduate from a university.

    a. an only

    b. the only

    c. one only

    d. only

18. "Did you meet Sally's niece at the company picnic?"

    "No, I came late, so I _____ her."

    a. didn't introduce

    b. wasn't introduced to

    c. couldn't introduce

    d. haven't introduced

19. Although Ted doesn't earn a high income, he _____ a very expensive neighborhood.

    a. lives in

    b. lives

    c. is to live with

    d. is living

20. Every time she wins some money, Sue _____ with her parents.

    a. shares the earnings

    b. is shared the earning

    c. sharing the earning

    d. has earned is shared

Vocabulary

Choose the word or phrase that best completes the sentence.

21. Your report would be easier to read if you _____ this part into two sections.

    a. crack

    b. split

    c. crash

    d. burst

22. After moving to a new city, it is normal to feel a little _____ at times.

    a. single

    b. lonely

    c. apart

    d. secluded

23. When Sam graduated from college, he was _____ for the opportunities his parents gave him.

    a. satisfied

    b. grateful

    c. thankless

    d. benefited

24. As a financial advisor, Marcia helps people to acquire and manage their _____.

    a. wealth

    b. purse

    c. means

    d. luxury

25. When a child misbehaves, everyone will think it is the parents' _____.

    a. blame

    b. lack

    c. flaw

    d. fault

26. Saving money is _____. Spend less than you earn.

    a. careless

    b. wieldy

    c. plain

    d. simple

27. Everyone worries when they are _____ and cannot sleep well at night.

    a. tense

    b. firm

    c. tight

    d. stiff

28. It is easy to _____ saving money with investing, because they are both important for financial planning.

    a. puzzle

    b. trouble

    c. confuse

    d. miscalculate

29. As people get older, they often begin to _____ their health and relationships more than money.

    a. devote

    b. admire

    c. value

    d. esteem

30. Couples that are _____ to each other's feelings are more likely to report being happy.

    a. thoughtful

    b. loving

    c. pitiful

    d. sensitive

Reading

Read the passage. Then answer the questions on page 83 according to the information given in the passage.

Having been popular for a long time in Europe, the gap year—an exploratory year off between high school and college—has been made world famous by British Princes William and Harry. During this year, young people get a clearer sense of purpose, gain the ability to manage money, and tend to be more focused on graduating college within four years. A non-profit educational organization reports that only 37 percent of all incoming freshmen in the United States achieve these outcomes.

Some young people volunteer, while others may travel as part of an organized program or on their own, or learn about a career by doing an internship or working full-time. Most schools recommend that gap year candidates apply to college while still in high school, rather than waiting until after their year off. Only once they have been admitted should they ask for a deferral. Many parents in the United States fear that if their children take a year off, they will not catch up with their peers in the job hunt or worse, that they will not go to college at all. However, recently many employers have come to look at the gap year as an advantage, not a drawback. Generally when students graduate, they lack experience. A gap year can be beneficial because almost all who take it gain a sense of financial, social, and intellectual maturity. These students are then better able to talk about their interests and accomplishments when interviewing and to have a better sense of what kind of career they want.

31. What is the main idea of the passage?

    a. to explain the gap year's popularity

    b. to discuss the value of the gap year

    c. to describe how to take a gap year

    d. to warn parents of gap year issues

32. What does the gap year provide incoming first-year students?

    a. an increased likelihood of graduating in four years

    b. an opportunity to meet famous people before college

    c. a chance to travel while studying in college

    d. an internship after completing their first year in college

33. According to the passage, what is the best approach for taking a gap year?

    a. get a job and then defer going to college

    b. apply to college after the gap year is over

    c. defer after getting admitted to college

    d. graduate from high school and wait a year

34. According to the passage, why isn't the gap year as popular in the United States as it is in Europe?

    a. Parents don't fully support it.

    b. Students cannot catch up with peers.

    c. Children refuse to go to college.

    d. Employers won't hire these students.

35. According to the passage, how do employers view the gap year?

    a. They gain maturity.

    b. They lack experience.

    c. It's a drawback.

    d. It's beneficial.

Reading—Part II

Answer the questions on page 85 according to the information provided in the ads.

①

Orlando Inn & Suites

We offer larger rooms, complimentary deluxe continental breakfast, and free scheduled shuttle service to all nearby theme parks. Jacuzzi and Kiddie Suites available.

④

Donner Suites & Hotel

Stay close to all major attractions. Two-room deluxe suites with complimentary breakfast buffet daily. Indoor and outdoor pools. Mention this ad for a free night.

②

FISHER RESORT

AND CONVENTION CENTER

Family vacation packages available year round.

Live in-house entertainment at the Fisher Theater.

Free airport shuttle daily.

③

Tropical Suites Orlando

All accommodations are deluxe suites with complimentary full breakfast, evening reception, free shuttle to theme parks and airport. We have two pools and cable TV. 15% off room rates with this ad.

⑤

Orlando Choice
VACATION HOMES

Luxury accommodations with private pools. This is your best choice for a great vacation in a home away from home. You have a great selection of the area's most desired homes and condos in beautiful locations. This will be a vacation your family will never forget!

36. Which place offers private pools?

    a. 2

    b. 3

    c. 4

    d. 5

37. Which vacation spot has a theater?

    a. 2

    b. 3

    c. 4

    d. 5

38. Which of the ads offer a special discount?

    a. 1 and 2

    b. 2 and 3

    c. 3 and 4

    d. 4 and 5

39. Which places provide free shuttle service?

    a. 1, 2, and 3

    b. 1, 2, and 4

    c. 1, 3, and 4

    d. 2, 3, and 4

40. Which locations offer free meals?

    a. 1, 2, and 3

    b. 1, 2, and 5

    c. 1, 3, and 4

    d. 2, 3, and 5

Ready to Handle Money?

Topic Discussion Activities

1. Small Group Discussion

In small groups, ask and answer the following questions.

1. How important is money in your life?

2. How does money affect relationships?

3. Would you date someone who doesn't have much money to spend?

4. Some people say that money brings happiness. Is that true for you?

2. Useful Expressions

Do you know these words? Use them to describe personal experiences.

Word Bank

Words Related to Money	
bills	a rip-off
buck	allowance
check	ATM
coins	cheap
currency	expensive
dime	inexpensive
nickel	money laundering
penny	salary
quarter	to rip off
	wage
	wealthy
	well off
	worthless

Idiomatic Expressions and Proverbs

What do these phrases mean? Work in pairs. Tell a story that illustrates one of these expressions. Your partner will guess which one you are referring to. Take turns.

A dime a dozen	To feel like a million dollars
To have money to burn	To tighten one's belt
Cash in your chips.	A fool and his money are soon parted.
Put your money where your mouth is.	To take a rain check
Time is money.	Money doesn't grow on trees.

3. Impromptu Short Speeches

Work in groups of three. Choose one of the idiomatic expressions in Activity 2B, and make a short speech. Everyone in the group will have two minutes to prepare these speeches. Your speech should have an interesting short title, a main point that can be said in one sentence, and at least two or three supporting points. All of you will have two minutes to deliver your speeches to the other two in the group.

Notes

_____

_____

_____

_____

_____

_____

_____

_____

ECCE Reading Practice

4. What Do You Think?

In small groups, discuss these questions. Do you agree with statement 1 or 2? Why? Talk to your partner about your opinion. Consider advantages and disadvantages of each situation.

1. Children should be given money to handle from an early age.

2. Children should not worry about handling money.

5. Scanning for Information

Read the following passage, and answer the questions. According to the author, how much money should a child receive

1. at the age of five? _____

2. at the age of ten? _____

Reading Passage

Read the passage, and then answer the questions on pages 91–93 according to the information given in the passage.

(1) Recently, an increasing number of advertisements have been targeting young children. Since schools typically do not teach personal finance in the classroom, parents need to teach their kids about money management at home. Today, 11 percent of teenagers and 76 percent of college students have credit cards. If they do not learn financial responsibility at a young age, many of these children may face a lifetime of uncontrolled debt as adults.

(2) Many financial experts recommend giving children the opportunity to learn to manage their money. From about age five, children should be given a small sum of money weekly as a toy and candy allowance. By age eight, a larger amount should be provided every two weeks. Then at ten, an even larger sum, which may include entertainment expenses, will be

deposited into a bank account at the end of the month. When children become teenagers, the amount of the allowance continues to grow and will cover clothing expenses as well.

(3) The reason for gradually increasing the time between payments with age is to ensure that children learn both the skills needed to make a budget and to "feel the pain" if they make mistakes. For example, a six-year-old may decide to spend his entire allowance on candy the day he or she gets the money, so that he or she has nothing left to buy ice cream later on that week. An older child may spend all his or her money on magazines and music CDs and then later cannot afford to go out to dinner or to see a movie with friends. Financial mistakes like these are important lessons for children, but they work only if parents cooperate by saying "no" when their kids ask for more money. If a parent gives in, then the children never really learn to make tough financial decisions.

(4) Some experts suggest that parents call this allowance a "salary," so that children begin to connect this money to the wages they will earn as future workers. Also, if children want extra money, they should be encouraged to work for it either by doing extra chores around the house or when older, by taking part-time jobs. As with all learning, children are bound to make some significant financial blunders; however, it isn't so bad when the mistakes are made while they are young and the sums are still fairly modest.

6. Checking Comprehension

Read the passage on pages 90 and 91 again. Answer the questions. Underline the text in the passage that contains information to answer these questions. Circle the letter of the best response.

1. How many college students have credit cards?

    a. those who are in debt

    b. around 10 percent

    c. the great majority

    d. a minority

2. Financial experts recommend

    a. giving children and teenagers a fixed amount of money every week

    b. increasing the amount of money parents give them every week

    c. giving more money less frequently

    d. increasing the amount of money and the time between payments

3. According to the article, a child at the age of five may get money to spend on

    a. toys or candy

    b. clothes and books

    c. school tuition

    d. entertainment

4. According to the article, how old should a child be to get enough money to buy his or her own clothes?

    a. five

    b. eight

    c. ten

    d. older than twelve

5. What should children do if they need money in addition to their allowance?

    a. ask their older brother or sister for more money

    b. do some more work around the home

    c. sell magazines

    d. get it from the bank account

6. When parents give in to children's demands, they are parents who probably

    a. punish their children

    b. give their children more money in addition to their allowance

    c. let their children buy more CDs than they should

    d. teach their children the value of money

7. Making mistakes with the money children get is

   a. significant experience for children

   b. good because they can ask for more money

   c. better than making mistakes at a later age

   d. bad for parents who want their children to be successful

7. Problem Solving

Read the following situation. What do you think the author would recommend to Jonathan's mother? What would you recommend?

Jonathan is 14 years old. He gets good grades, and every time he gets an A and tells his mother, she gives him $25. He has been getting home late after school because he has been going to a friend's house to study with him. This week, another student called Jonathan's mother because Jonathan has been playing cards for money, and the student said Jonathan owes him more than $300.

The author suggests . . .	I suggest . . .

ECCE Language Practice

8. Vocabulary: Matching

Match the words from the reading in the left column with synonyms (words or phrases) in the right column.

1. target	a. household tasks, responsibilities
2. wages	b. guarantee, make certain
3. blunders	c. horrifying, inexcusable, terrible
4. give in	d. objective, aim
5. ensure	e. income, earning
6. earn	f. make money
7. appalling	g. mistakes, errors
8. chores	h. comply, concede, surrender, yield

9. Grammar: Phrasal Verbs

Choose the answer that is closest in meaning to the underlined expression.

1. Nobody thought that Paula and Jason would ever <u>break up</u>.

    a. They are together and became friends.

    b. They were dating and are now separated.

    c. They broke a window and entered a house to steal.

    d. They escaped from school together.

2. After arguing for hours about where to go on their honeymoon, Alan <u>gave in</u>.

    a. He won. His fiancée will accept what he proposed.

    b. He suggested a new place.

    c. He accepted what his fiancée proposed.

    d. He decided he doesn't want to get married.

3. Nobody expected that Jason himself would <u>call on</u> us this late.

    a. Jason phoned us.

    b. Jason shouted at us.

    c. Jason canceled his appointment.

    d. Jason visited us.

4. Sheila can't <u>make out</u> what the teacher wants.

    a. She can't understand the teacher.

    b. She can't invent a story for the teacher.

    c. She refused the teacher's invitation.

    d. She can't do her homework.

5. You won't believe who I just <u>ran across</u> in the parking lot.

    a. I had an accident and hit someone.

    b. I had an appointment.

    c. I met someone I didn't expect.

    d. I was approached by a stranger.

6. I didn't expect anyone would <u>turn down</u> my bid.

    a. The volume was too high.

    b. The bid was not accepted.

    c. The bid was accepted.

    d. The bidder suddenly appeared.

7. Everybody says that Matt <u>takes after</u> his father.

    a. He takes care of his father.

    b. He is very close to his father.

    c. He is very similar to his father.

    d. He is trying to control his father.

8. To get along with my dad, you'd better not <u>put off</u> anything he wants.

    a. Don't postpone things.

    b. Don't criticize him.

    c. Don't annoy him.

    d. Don't buy everything he asks for.

10. Grammar: Conditional Clauses

Complete the following sentences. Then read the full sentences to your partner.

<u>Example:</u>

If I won a million dollars, <u>I would donate all of it to charity.</u>

1. If I could go back to a special moment in my childhood, _____

   _____.

2. If I had paid attention to the advice I received, _____

   _____.

3. If I were younger and stronger, _____

   _____.

4. If we have time during the weekend, _____

   _____.

5. We will help a homeless family if _____

   _____.

6. I would be living in another place today if _____

   _____.

7. I could've made that decision much earlier if _____

   _____.

8. I wouldn't be the person that I am today unless _____

   _____.

11. Grammar: Adverbial Clauses

Complete the sentences with the correct adverbial clause. Pay attention to verb tenses to use. One has been done for you.

Spending Family Time

1. My best friend will get together with all his extended family this weekend in order

   that _they can celebrate his grandfather's 85th birthday._____

2. In the event that we need to be reached while we are on vacation, _____

   _____.

3. We always have fun at our family dinners provided that _____

   _____.

4. I remember that we used to treat my youngest cousin as though _____

   _____.

5. We try to get a variety of board games and fun activities, so that _____

   _____.

6. Some families try to spend lots of time together as long as _____

   _____. Others, however, _____.

7. It's important for everyone in the family to know the reasons why _____

   _____.

8. Grandma often tries to run to the kitchen as soon as _____

   _____.

9. Whenever we can, _____.

10. Whereas my mother's family _____, _____

    _____.

12. Grammar: Indefinite Pronouns and Quantifiers

Choose the correct option. Explain to a partner why the others are incorrect.

1. There were _____ coins on top of the dresser. It was enough to pay for the bus ticket.

   a. any

   b. a little

   c. much

   d. a few

2. Jimmy _____ to get an allowance yet.

   a. is enough old

   b. is old

   c. isn't old enough

   d. is too old

3. I can't believe there aren't _____ banks open after 6:00 PM around here.

   a. a

   b. any

   c. not

   d. the

4. "How _____ did you deposit in the account today?"

   "Oh, less than $50."

   a. much

   b. many

   c. less

   d. few

5. We have _____ cash left. We will need to get some more from the bank before we take the bus.

   a. little

   b. the little

   c. few

   d. the few

6. We only need to wait _____ minutes before the bank opens.

   a. more few

   b. any more

   c. a little more

   d. a few more

13. Sentence Completion

After completing the sentences, read them aloud to a partner. What are the most original ideas from your group?

1. One dollar is enough to get _____, but the

   best you can get for $1 is _____.

2. The best meal you can get for under $3 is _____

   _____.

3. The most expensive restaurant I ever went to was _____

   _____.

4. The nicest and cheapest clothes I ever bought were _____

   _____.

5. The most embarrassing moment when paying for a bill was when _____

   _____.

6. Stingy people are _____.

7. The most generous person I know is _____

   _____.

8. If you want good deals, you ought to _____.

ECCE Writing Practice

THE ANN ARBOR TIMES

Ethics in Advertising. Children are the target of many commercials and advertisements on TV, radio, in magazines, and on the Internet. Companies that sell toys, computer games, music CDs, or even clothes want children to know about their products. In this way, children will convince their parents to buy more things. For many people, this is an unethical way of selling products. *The Ann Arbor Times* wants to know your opinion.

14. Writing Exercises

Choose one of the task options.

A. *Letter to the Editor*

Write a letter to the editor of *The Ann Arbor Times*. Explain whether or not you think companies should target children in their advertising campaigns. Give specific examples in your letter.

B. *Essay*

Some companies only want to sell more products and do not care how they increase their sales. Which advertising or marketing practices should not be considered legal? Illustrate your point with specific examples.

ECCE Listening Practice

15. Listening: Short Conversations

After each conversation, a question is asked about what was heard. The possible answers to the question are shown as pictures. Circle the correct answer for each question. Remember that each conversation is heard only once. Conversations are not repeated.

ECCE Speaking Practice

16. Offering Advice

Work in pairs. One of you will look at the information in Box A, and the other one will look at the information in Box B (page 155). A will ask B questions to find out more about the problem. Then A needs to offer B some advice.

What advice can you offer? Why did you choose that option? Why didn't you choose the other one? *Make sure you use some of the information that B mentioned in your answer.*

A. Your friend has a decision to make. Ask questions to find out what the problem is and offer your advice.

Look at the pictures and ask:
- Who is this person?
- What is the problem?
- What are the possible solutions?
- What are the advantages and disadvantages of each solution?

17. Elaboration Questions

With a partner, ask each other these questions. Try to spend at least two minutes responding to each question. Encourage each other to develop the topic. Pay attention to the level of detail when elaborating.

1. Would you ever borrow money from a friend? Do you know of others who have done so?

2. What are some ways in which people behave when they owe money?

3. How can money problems affect relationships with friends or family?

Family and Relationships

Topic Discussion Activities

1. Hobbies and Pastimes

What is the difference between a hobby and a pastime? Look at the list, and check the hobbies or pastimes that you have had or would like to have.

antiques
arts and crafts
astronomy
baking
bird watching
carpentry
cars
collecting
computing and the Internet
contests
cooking
crafts
crossword puzzles
dance classes
dolls
drawing

fishing	magic	reading
flying	models and miniatures	sculpting
games	movies	shopping
gardening	music	singing
ham radio	newspapers and magazines	sports
horseback riding	performing arts	teddy bears
hunting	photography	TV
kites	pottery	toys
leisure activities	puzzles	writing

2. Small Group Discussion

In small groups, discuss the following questions.

1. What kind of hobbies or pastimes do you think members of your family from different generations were interested in?

2. What might you be able to tell about a person from the hobbies or pastimes that he or she has?

3. How can hobbies or pastimes affect family or social life positively or negatively?

3. Favorite Places

Make a list of five favorite places you used to visit when you were younger. Write the name of the people who were with you. Tell your partner about these memories and what made them special.

My favorite places were . . .	I was with . . .	These moments were special because . . .

ECCE Reading Practice 1

Reading Passage 1

Read the passage, and then answer the questions on page 107 according to the information given in the passage.

It is charming to watch otherwise articulate adults talk to infants. They babble and coo. New research in the United States reveals that this baby talk actually helps to develop the skills needed for language learning. In one study, 40 babies between the ages of 6½ and 7½ months listened to a set of nonsense words spoken in two different ways. In one version, the nonsense words were spoken in high-pitched, exaggerated tones that resembled baby talk. In the other, the same words were delivered in a normal adult monotone style. It was found that not only did the babies listen longer to the words that were delivered in baby talk, but that the baby talk likely also helped the infants to focus on the sound of the words and, ultimately, learn to imitate the rhythm of sentences.

One researcher explains, "A small difference in the speed of language learning from the beginning can make a big difference in later development. We know that one-year-old children who have been exposed to greater amounts of baby talk tend to have noticeably better speech perception skills than those who haven't." However, experts agree that any time parents spend talking with their children is important. To make the most of these interactions, it is important for parents to maintain eye contact as much as possible. Another key language development skill is learning to participate and take turns. When the baby pauses, the parent responds to teach the baby how to time interactions. Parents can respond to gestures by describing both the objects and the actions, such as when the baby points to an object and the parent asks, "Do you want the ball?" Parents can benefit from both research and tips from experts to give their children an edge in learning to speak.

4. Checking Comprehension

Read the passage on page 106 again. Answer the questions. Underline the text in the passage that contains the information to answer these questions. Circle the letter of the best response.

1. Babbling and cooing are

   a. characteristic of adult speech

   b. harmful for babies

   c. examples of baby talk

   d. monotonous ways of talking

2. In the study reported in the readings,

   a. babies who speak earlier pay more attention when listening

   b. babies heard new words in two different ways

   c. 20 babies were exposed to another language for 6–7 months

   d. 40 babies talked and were recorded

3. The study reported that babies who listened to baby talk

   a. speak in a monotone as adults

   b. pay more attention to the sound of new words

   c. sing rather than read sentences

   d. comprehend longer sentences easily

4. According to the passage, what is the most important factor in helping children learn to speak?

   a. show their children how to express opinions since the age of one

   b. interact with children, using appropriate eye contact

   c. describe actions when children want to play

   d. spend time with children and teach them adult language

5. Who is the intended audience of this reading?

   a. parents

   b. medical doctors

   c. infants and children

   d. researchers

Reading Passage 2

Answer the questions on pages 109 and 110 according to the information provided in the ads.

Kiddie Land Toy Store

One-stop shop for toys, books, videos/DVDs, and video games.

We have everything you need to plan your next birthday party!

Show this ad and get 15% off your next purchase.

Hobby House

We have the best selection of model trains, planes, and cars in town.

We have everything you need for any art or craft project imaginable: glue, paint, wood. . . .

If we don't have it, we'll get it for you!

Get your Hobby House membership card. It's free, and you get 10% off every time you show your card.

Hands-on
Science Museum

Spend the day having fun and learning about science.

Every Saturday at 11:00 AM, a university professor gives a short lecture to the kids.

Entry Fee:

$10 for one adult 18 and older

$5 for a child 5 to 17 years old

Free for children 4 and under

Buy a one-year Family Membership and get unlimited entry into the Museum for the entire family and up to four guests at one time. Just $100 per year. School groups admitted free.

Second Childhood

We buy and sell gently used clothing, toys, and more. We have baby gear, including cribs, high chairs, strollers, and car seats.

On the 2nd of every month, we offer 50% off any item marked with a red tag.

Art Zone

Learn to paint, draw, sculpt clay, act, and dance. We have classes for all abilities and ages from toddlers to retirees. Our school shop has all the materials, equipment, clothing you need for class or other projects. Each 10-session course is $75; our members' rate is $50. Annual Art Zone memberships are available for $100 for individuals and $150 for families.

5. Scanning for Information

Answer the questions according to the information provided in the ads on page 108. Numbers correspond to ad numbers.

1. You want to buy a toy train for your nephew. Which places might have one?

    a. 1 and 2

    b. 1 and 3

    c. 2 and 3

    d. 1, 2, and 3

2. You are preparing a surprise party for a friend. Where might you find party hats and decorations?

    a. 1 and 5

    b. 2 and 3

    c. Only 1

    d. Only 3

3. You are taking two neighbors to the Hands-on Science Museum where you are a member. They are three and seven years old. How much do you have to pay to get in?

    a. $10

    b. $15

    c. $20

    d. $25

4. Where can you become a member by paying an annual fee?

    a. 1 and 2

    b. 1 and 3

    c. 2, 3, and 4

    d. 3, 4, and 5

5. If you have $50 to use at these businesses, what could you buy with it (using all $50)?

    a. ten dancing lessons at Art Zone, if you have an annual membership

    b. an individual membership at the museum

    c. unlimited painting lessons at Art Zone

    d. five children's entrance fees to the museum

6. How many people can be admitted to the museum with the annual Family Membership pass?

   a. maximum of five people

   b. eight people

   c. parents and children

   d. one adult and one child under four

7. If you are not a member of the Art Zone but would like to take a course, how much do you have to pay?

   a. $50

   b. $75

   c. $100

   d. $150

8. On which day(s) can you take your children to a lecture at the museum?

   a. on Sunday

   b. on Saturdays

   c. on weekdays

   d. on Mondays

9. Which place offers special discounts when you present its ad?

   a. 1

   b. 2

   c. 3

   d. 4

10. How much does a group of ten students have to pay if they go with their teacher to the museum?

    a. $20

    b. $50

    c. $100

    d. nothing

ECCE Language Practice

6. Vocabulary: Associated Words

Cross out the word that does not belong in each group. Then explain what the group has in common on the blank.

a. sketch	sculpt	draw	paint	_____
b. lecture	retiree	senior	elderly	_____
c. membership	ticket	fee	exit	_____
d. buy	purchase	lease	acquire	_____
e. stroller	pacifier	crib	bike	_____
f. toddler	infant	sibling	child	_____

7. Grammar: Review of Verb Tenses and Modal Auxiliaries

The following sentences are part of one conversation. Choose the answer that completes the statement.

1. "How long _____ together with grandpa?"

   "Ohh! More than 65 years! I think we are getting old now."

   a. were you

   b. are you

   c. did you be

   d. have you been

2. "As a matter of fact, next May we _____ for exactly 68 years."

   a. will marry

   b. will have married

   c. will have been married

   d. will get married

3. "We _____ classmates in junior high before we met again in college."

   a. were

   b. had been

   c. have been

   d. haven't been

4. "We _____ in the same house for more than 40 years."

   a. live

   b. had lived

   c. have been living

   d. are living

5. "Grandma, you _____ many exciting experiences together."

   a. should have had

   b. must have had

   c. may have

   d. ought to have

6. "Yes. I remember we _____ on the deck of a cruise in the Caribbean once when a storm hit our ship. It was the scariest experience I ever had."

   a. were lying

   b. laid

   c. would be lying

   d. lie

7. "Right now, I only wish I _____ back to the day we got married! I'd like to relive that day again."

   a. were going

   b. had gone

   c. could go

   d. should go

8. "We have been to so many places together. In fact, we are now planning a trip to the Amazon. In a few weeks we _____ in the jungle with a native guide. It will be fascinating."

   a. have walked

   b. ought to be walked

   c. will have walked

   d. will be walking

9. "Do you have any advice for me, Grandma?"

   "You _____ follow your heart. That's what worked best for me."

   a. would

   b. had to

   c. must

   d. must have

8. Grammar: Discourse Markers

Complete the sentences with one of your own ideas. Read them aloud to a partner.

1. I get along very well with my _____. In fact, _____

   _____.

2. We can spend a lot of time together; furthermore, we even _____

   _____.

3. Whenever I need someone to talk to, I look for _____. However,

   _____.

4. Having a lot of good friends is not an easy thing. Actually, _____

   _____.

5. I need to spend at least one day a week with my friends. Nevertheless, _____

   _____.

6. Many people don't know how important a good friend can be to have. Consequently,

   _____.

9. Grammar: Prepositions

Complete the sentences with the correct preposition.

1. My cousin Jessie was born _____ Milwaukee, Wisconsin, _____ July 24, 1985.

2. He has a degree _____ marketing and works _____ an international food company.

3. Ever since he was hired, he has been dreaming _____ becoming the president of the company.

4. He fell in love _____ one of his assistants. Actually, she is the love _____ his life.

5. The problem with becoming company president is that he seems to depend _____ her for any decision he needs to make.

6. She has turned him _____ her slave. He will do _____ her whatever she wants.

7. It seems he can't discriminate _____ what is right and wrong if she is not _____ him.

8. I hope that he is able to gain confidence _____ her to go _____ his dream.

10. Grammar: Phrasal Verbs

Use these verb-preposition combinations and make up a story based on your experience or that of any of your acquaintances.

break up	make up
bring up	put up with
look after	take after

_____

_____

_____

_____

_____

_____

_____

_____

ECCE Writing Practice

THE ANN ARBOR TIMES

Parents vs. Peers. A recent survey shows that teenagers nowadays learn a lot more from their peers and friends than from their parents. It seems that parents are spending much less time with their teenagers, leaving the education of teens to other sources. If you could change anything about how teenagers are educated today, what would you like to change? *The Ann Arbor Times* wants to know your opinion.

---

11. Writing Exercises

Choose one of the task options.

A. *Letter to the Editor*

Write a letter to the editor of *The Ann Arbor Times* about the age or ages you think it is okay for children to be left unsupervised at home, and under what circumstance.

B. *Essay*

Parents are often accused in the media of being either overprotective or neglectful of their children. How do you think parents can best help their children become responsible, independent adults?

ECCE Listening Practice

12. Listening: Radio Interview

Imagine you are listening to the radio. You are going to hear someone from a radio station interviewing one or more people at a special event. You will hear the interview in several parts. After each part, you will hear some questions. There are three answer choices for each question. You should select, from the three answer choices, the best answer to the question. If you want to, you may take notes as you listen.

Remember, after each section of the interview, you will hear some questions. On the test, the sections are separated by double lines. On the test, you will have 12 seconds to mark your answer by circling the letter of the best response.

Segment 1:

1. a. more than 1,200 people

   b. 1,200 people exactly

   c. fewer than 1,200 people

2. a. The Expo begins tomorrow.

   b. It's the first day.

   c. It's the second day.

3. a. new mothers

   b. new fathers

   c. all parents

4. a. there was a lot of information for them

   b. he knew what it was like to be one

   c. there were many new books for men

5. a. they have many fears in common

   b. they are experts in taking care of infants

   c. they read a lot of books written for them

Notes about Segment 1:

Segment 2:   *Notes about Segment 2:*

6. a. being a good father

   b. not having enough money

   c. not being relaxed around the
      baby

7. a. It's the only way to become an
      expert overnight.

   b. He is more likely to spend one-
      on-one time with the baby.

   c. Often he is the only person
      earning money in the family.

8. a. to be comfortable being with the
      baby

   b. to keep track of how much
      money is spent

   c. to earn enough money to afford
      the new baby

ECCE Speaking Practice

13. Offering Advice

Work in pairs. One of you will look at the information in Box A, and the other one will look at the information in Box B (on page 155). A will ask B questions to find out more about the problem. Then A needs to offer B some advice.

Once you have enough information, offer your advice. You can choose one of these options or make up your own. Why did you choose that option? Why didn't you choose the other one? *Make sure you use some of the information that B mentioned in your answer.*

A. Your friend has a decision to make. Ask questions to find out what the problem is and offer your advice.

Look at the pictures and ask:
- Who is this person?
- What is the problem?
- What are the possible solutions?
- What are the advantages and disadvantages of each solution?

14. Elaboration Questions

With a partner, ask each other these questions. Try to spend at least three minutes responding to each question. Encourage each other to develop the topic. Pay attention to the level of detail when elaborating.

1. How important is being open and honest with your friends?

2. How different is your relationship with your family from your relationship with your friends?

3. Who do you turn to when you have problems?

4. Would any of your friends ask you for advice if they have any difficulties? Why?

ECCE Full Test/Practice Test

Listening Test—Part I
INSTRUCTIONS

DO NOT BEGIN THIS SECTION UNTIL THE EXAMINER HAS READ THESE INSTRUCTIONS WITH YOU.

This is a test of your ability to understand spoken English. You will hear short conversations. After you hear each conversation, you will be asked a question about what you heard. The answer choices are shown as pictures. Mark your answers on the separate answer sheet. Do not write in the test booklet. Here is an example.

<u>Example:</u>

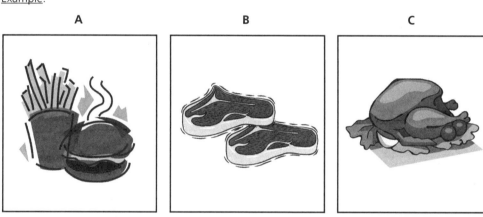

A   B   C

The correct answer is C, because they will make roasted chicken with a large green salad for dinner. The woman had steak for lunch. The man ate a hamburger and fries for his lunch.

You will hear each conversation only once; they will not be repeated. Please be very quiet and listen carefully. Remember to mark all your answers on the separate answer sheet. You should mark A, B, or C. There will be 30 questions in Part I.

Do you have any questions before you begin?

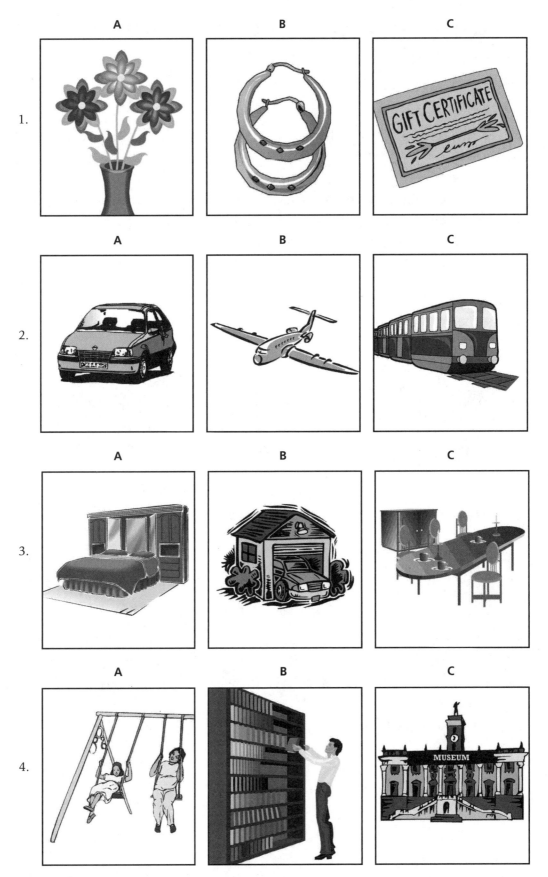

This is only a practice test © 2006.

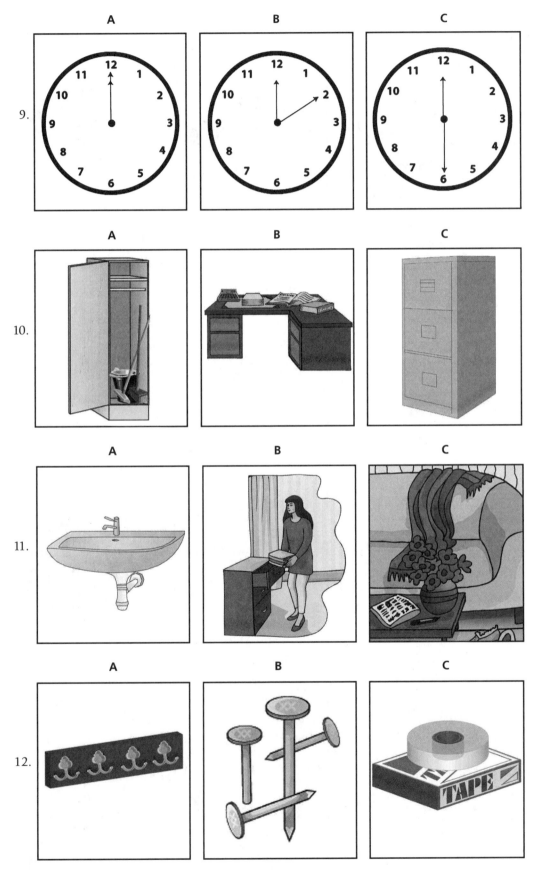

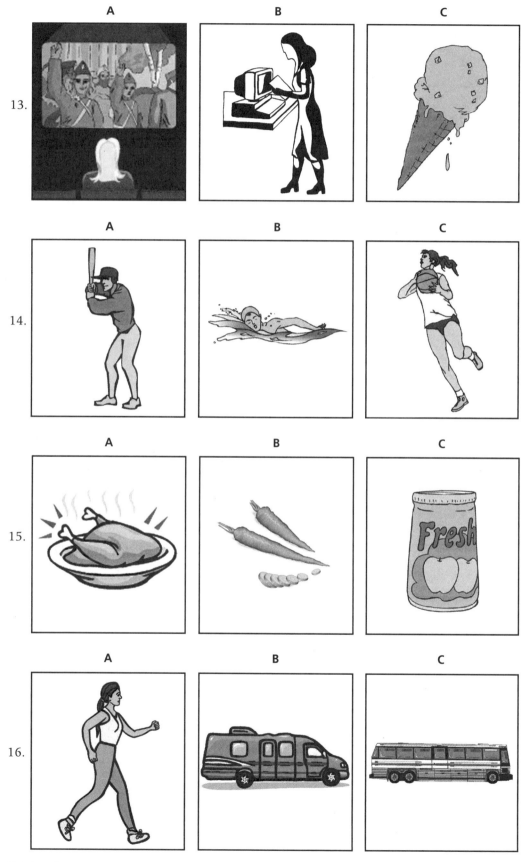

This is only a practice test © 2006.

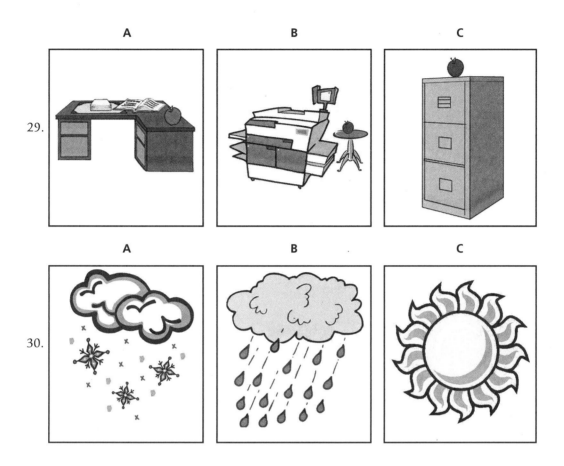

29.

A B C

30.

A B C

End of Part I of the Listening Test

Listening Test—Part II

Imagine you are listening to the radio. You are going to hear someone from a radio station interviewing three people at a special event.

- First, you will hear general information about this event.

- Then, you will hear from someone at the event.

- Next, you will hear from a psychologist.

- Finally, you will hear from a financial advisor.

You will hear the interview in several parts. After each part, you will hear some questions. There are three answer choices for each question. You should select, from the three answer choices, the best answer to the question. If you want to, you may take notes below as you listen.

Now you will hear the beginning of the first interview. For this part, there will not be any actual test questions. The questions that follow this part are examples only.

Example 1:

A. at the airport

B. at a radio station

C. at an expo

The correct answer is C, at an expo.

Example 2:

A. a team of people

B. the organizer

C. a visitor

The correct answer is B, the organizer.

Now we will continue this interview. Remember, after each section of the interview you will hear some questions. In the test booklet, the sections are separated by double lines. On the test, you will have 12 seconds to mark your answer to each question. Mark your answers on the separate answer sheet. There will be 20 questions. Are there any questions before we begin?

Segment 1:

31. A. secrets

    B. money

    C. health

32. A. New York City

    B. Chicago

    C. Los Angeles

33. A. 22%

    B. 60%

    C. 81%

34. A. being happy

    B. worrying

    C. lacking control

Notes about Segment 1:

Segment 2:

35. A. a million dollars

    B. $50,000

    C. It's not a dollar amount; depends on other factors.

36. A. They are dependent on factors that can change.

    B. They depend on earning levels.

    C. They are related to the amount of savings.

37. A. how to live like a millionaire

    B. how to gain control over their finances

    C. how to earn more money

Notes about Segment 2:

This is only a practice test © 2006.

Segment 2:

38. A. less than $42,000

    B. more than $42,000

    C. above $50,000

Notes about Segment 2 (cont.):

Segment 3:

Notes about Segment 3:

39. A. a lack of control over money

    B. gaining a sense of control

    C. just having little things

40. A. finding the biggest differences

    B. buying special furniture

    C. creating a way to be organized

41. A. little things

    B. less frustration

    C. losing time

42. A. Overall you spend less time doing this task.

    B. It's a quicker way to find your bills.

    C. People feel hopeless when they pay bills.

43. A. Knowing helps make people happier.

    B. It's awful to pay bills all at once.

    C. It helps to hire a professional organizer.

Segment 4:   *Notes about Segment 4:*

44. A. a simple way to save money

    B. being sensible about investing

    C. a feeling of being in control

45. A. 5% of household income

    B. $4 a day

    C. about $1,500 a year

46. A. how to be in a strong
        relationship

    B. finding free coffee

    C. seeing expensive habits

47. A. They want a special treat.

    B. They want to save money.

    C. It costs too much money.

Segment 5:   *Notes about Segment 5:*

48. A. Less fighting makes people
        happier.

    B. You can spend more to be
        happy.

    C. Your spouse will have more
        money.

49. A. stopping a fight about money

    B. creating financial goals

    C. donating time or money

50. A. communicating about money

    B. saving for a shared goal

    C. giving money to a charity you
        believe in

End of the Listening Test

Grammar   Vocabulary   Reading
INSTRUCTIONS

DO NOT BEGIN THIS SECTION UNTIL THE EXAMINER HAS READ THESE INSTRUCTIONS WITH YOU.

1. There are 100 problems in this section of the examination. There are grammar, vocabulary, and reading problems. They are numbered 51 through 150. Examples of each kind of problem are given below.

2. You will have 80 minutes to finish the entire Grammar, Vocabulary, Reading (GVR) section. Try to answer all the problems. Do not spend too much time on any one problem or you will not have time to finish this section. You may answer the problems in any order you wish.

3. Each problem in this section has only one correct answer. Completely fill in the circle that corresponds to the answer you have chosen. Do not make any stray marks on your answer sheet. If you change your mind about an answer, erase your first mark completely. Any problem with more than one answer marked will be counted as wrong. If you are not sure about an answer, you may guess.

4. Here are examples of each kind of problem. In each example, the correct answer has been underlined. For the actual problems, fill in the circle of the correct answer. Do not mark your answers in this test booklet.

Grammar

Choose the word or phrase that best completes the sentence or the conversation.

That thing _____ a spider

    a. to call

    b. calls

    c. called

    <u>d. is called</u>

"What is that thing?"

"That _____ a spider."

    a. to call

    b. calls

    c. called

    <u>d. is called</u>

This is only a practice test © 2006.

Vocabulary

Choose the word or phrase that most appropriately completes the sentence.

Can you _____ me what time it is?

    a. give

    <u>b.</u> <u>tell</u>

    c. call

    d. say

Reading

There are three kinds of reading passages. In one kind, you will read the passage first, then answer the questions following it according to the information given in the passage. In the other two, you will read the questions first, then look in the text on the facing page for answers. This example question might accompany a brochure about musical events in a city:

If you want to buy a ticket for the holiday concert, you should . . .

    a. call 763–0500.

    b. order them by mail.

    <u>c.</u> <u>go to the theater office.</u>

    d. contact your local high school.

5. Remember you have 80 minutes to finish the entire GVR section. Do not write in the test booklet. Mark only on the answer sheet. You may begin now.

This is only a practice test © 2006.

Grammar Items

51. "Was Jim able to get into the higher-level course?"

    "Yes, but he needs to _____ to keep up with the other students."

    a. studying harder

    b. harder study

    c. hard study

    d. study hard

52. The students have a few choices for a class party; _____ are expensive, and others are not.

    a. some

    b. both

    c. ones

    d. all

53. "Did you start work right after graduation?"

    "Yes, and _____ I have been with the same company."

    a. until then

    b. since then

    c. then now

    d. until now

54. The counselor can see you _____ you are available.

    a. anytime

    b. anyhow

    c. anything

    d. anyways

55. Mary thought well of _____ for the school newsletter.

    a. I was writing

    b. my writing

    c. writing myself

    d. I wrote

56. Diane hasn't decided whether or not _____ the job offer in California.

    a. she will be taking

    b. she will to take

    c. she has taken

    d. to have to take

57. The lawyer asked many questions to check that _____ correct.

    a. all facts were

    b. facts all were

    c. all facts

    d. facts were all

58. Unlike for a typical class quiz, Steve studied _____ possible for the final exam.

    a. the most

    b. more than

    c. as much as

    d. much more than

59. Sarah's boyfriend willingly did _____ she asked of him.

    a. whenever

    b. wherever

    c. whatever

    d. however

60. "What do you think is the best way to learn a new language?"

    "Besides studying in class, I recommend that you _____ a short dialogue each week."

    a. memorize

    b. having memorized

    c. memorizing

    d. have memorized

61. While looking _____ the children, the babysitter took them to the park.

    a. away

    b. after

    c. over

    d. toward

62. "Kate offered to create a new filing system."

    "It's fantastic. How did she manage to organize _____?"

    a. everything so carefully

    b. everything so careful

    c. careful everything

    d. carefully so everything

63. The other day the fog was very thick, _____ it difficult to drive.

    a. to make

    b. making

    c. makes

    d. made

64. It's not easy to win the contest, but she will try _____.

    a. furthermore

    b. nonetheless

    c. consequently

    d. moreover

65. Cindy didn't want _____ how much she spent shopping last month.

    a. her husband to know

    b. to know her husband

    c. her husband being known

    d. to be known her husband

66. It would be better to paint the house now _____ wait for the winter.

    a. rather

    b. other that

    c. other than

    d. than to

67. Christina doesn't need _____ until she is ready to open a beauty salon.

    a. to get her license

    b. her license to be gotten

    c. getting her license

    d. her license being gotten

68. To complete the report before going home last night, Jane _____ to drink strong coffee throughout the day.

    a. should have

    b. was having

    c. had

    d. has had

69. I went to the dentist on Monday because I _____ a tooth over the weekend.

    a. was breaking

    b. had to break

    c. had broken

    d. was to break

70. "Has Sandy finished grilling the hamburgers for the picnic?"

    "No, she's still got a long _____ before finishing."

    a. way to go

    b. ways going

    c. way they go

    d. way she goes

71. In the past 20 years, _____ to communicate has changed dramatically.

    a. our ability

    b. we have the ability

    c. the ability of us

    d. ability of ours

72. Who is interested _____ developing this idea for the next meeting?

    a. by

    b. for

    c. in

    d. of

73. My car will not start. I've tried everything and still can't find _____ is wrong.

    a. what

    b. how

    c. that

    d. which

74. My brother told me _____ to select the best computer for my needs.

    a. what

    b. how

    c. which

    d. that

75. Come September, I _____ at the university for five years.

    a. am working

    b. will work

    c. have worked

    d. will have worked

76. I can't believe our teacher _____ a report that's due tomorrow.

    a. we asked to write

    b. asked us to write

    c. we asked to be writing

    d. asks us to have written

77. "What's the matter? Are you sick?"

    "No, I'm ____ tired. I need to go to sleep early tonight."

    a. even

    b. just

    c. some

    d. such

78. Linda was committed to ending the dispute ____ her boss and her co-workers.

    a. within

    b. around

    c. between

    d. inside of

79. After losing 20 pounds, Peter has ____ he is training to run a marathon.

    a. that much energy more

    b. that so much more energy

    c. so much energy more that

    d. so much more energy that

80. When the next board meeting ____, the members will vote on the proposal.

    a. held

    b. is holding

    c. to be held

    d. is held

81. ____ you become a regular customer, you will find you get better service.

    a. How

    b. When

    c. So that

    d. For

82. Larry's parents were ____ when he won the statewide tournament in debate.

    a. impressive

    b. impressed

    c. impressing

    d. impression

83. I wanted to discuss with you the latest report ____ you wrote.

    a. that

    b. of which

    c. what

    d. of that

84. My second cousins ____ my father's side live in Ireland.

    a. at

    b. by

    c. in

    d. on

85. When looking for a new job, it's important to weigh the salary and the working conditions ____.

    a. equal

    b. equaled

    c. equally

    d. equality

Vocabulary Items

86. Heather has an annoying _____ of biting her fingernails.

   a. manner

   b. habit

   c. custom

   d. turn

87. Because of the flu, many students were _____ from class today.

   a. left

   b. abroad

   c. lost

   d. absent

88. The opposing team was _____ to use the mistake to their advantage.

   a. quick

   b. hasty

   c. brisk

   d. speedy

89. After a thorough discussion, they _____ to hire someone with more experience.

   a. settled

   b. concluded

   c. decided

   d. selected

90. If you _____ carefully, you will hear a strange sound in the engine.

   a. overhear

   b. detect

   c. attend

   d. listen

91. Summer is the best time to visit Michigan. The bright sunny days make the _____ countryside look even better.

   a. beautiful

   b. attractive

   c. good-looking

   d. handsome

92. Children age two and under may travel _____ when accompanied by an adult.

   a. ideal

   b. clear

   c. free

   d. loose

93. Now that we are expecting a baby, I am starting to _____ getting a new job.

   a. suppose

   b. consider

   c. acknowledge

   d. determine

94. Before starting the construction project, the engineers inspected all of the building _____.

   a. materials

   b. provisions

   c. ingredients

   d. fractions

95. All passengers are required to _____ their seatbelts before the aircraft takes off.

    a. unite

    b. fasten

    c. adhere

    d. bind

96. That shelf is too _____ to hold these potted plants.

    a. dim

    b. vague

    c. lacking

    d. weak

97. It is a tradition that the winner of the talent show _____ the following year's contest.

    a. awards

    b. resolves

    c. examines

    d. judges

98. Margaret _____ to catch the first train to arrive at work early, but she woke up late.

    a. advised

    b. intended

    c. affected

    d. designed

99. Since we are short one person today, there will be a _____ change of plans.

    a. petty

    b. slight

    c. petite

    d. flimsy

100. The president's emotional speech had a great _____ on the subsequent vote.

    a. influence

    b. essence

    c. response

    d. interest

101. There will be an airline strike if management does not agree to the pilots' _____ for a pay increase.

    a. order

    b. demand

    c. command

    d. rule

102. Our two-year-old son will _____ his fork in either hand when he eats.

    a. make

    b. gain

    c. occupy

    d. hold

103. The main office will move from its more _____ location downtown to a larger site just outside of the city.

    a. compound

    b. complex

    c. charitable

    d. central

104. Please remind me that I still _____ my share of the retirement gift for John.

    a. owe

    b. pay

    c. lend

    d. save

This is only a practice test © 2006.

105. University career services offers practical _____ for seniors searching for employment.

    a. presentation

    b. guidance

    c. stability

    d. concentration

106. If Jim wins this competition, he will become the fifth- _____ golfer in the state.

    a. degree

    b. class

    c. ranked

    d. ordered

107. As Andrew's illness worsened, he gained an increasing _____ of sympathy from students and teachers at his school.

    a. number

    b. result

    c. total

    d. amount

108. It's a _____ suggestion to get a second opinion before signing a legal contract.

    a. secure

    b. stable

    c. steady

    d. sensible

109. Whenever Tom needs a break from big city life, he likes to get back in touch with _____ by camping in the mountains.

    a. landscape

    b. nature

    c. outdoors

    d. environment

110. Our professional association will not use this conference site again. There have been more than 100 _____ about the service and the facility.

    a. complaints

    b. objections

    c. reviews

    d. confessions

111. The customer lost his _____ with the waiter after being served the wrong order three times.

    a. modesty

    b. regret

    c. patience

    d. concern

112. Since I was asked to keep this information secret, I was _____ not to talk about this topic.

    a. composed

    b. careful

    c. reckless

    d. thorough

113. Since I planned to work in a multi-national corporation, I took several college courses on the history and politics of foreign _____ and international relations.

    a. trade

    b. enterprise

    c. sales

    d. professions

114. This breed can be trained to be fierce watchdogs, but when they are puppies they are quite _____.

    a. careless

    b. thoughtless

    c. regardless

    d. harmless

115. After working nonstop for a week to meet the deadline, you _____ to rest over the weekend.

    a. deserve

    b. merit

    c. earn

    d. warrant

116. I could make out two or three _____ in the fog, but I couldn't tell who they were.

    a. masses

    b. structures

    c. outlines

    d. figures

117. When Sam started this business 20 years ago, he had little money and needed to _____ a large sum from the bank.

    a. rent

    b. adopt

    c. borrow

    d. loan

118. There has been such _____ competition for this job that the hiring committee still hasn't selected the top candidates yet.

    a. spiked

    b. keen

    c. vivid

    d. harsh

119. I felt deeply _____ when Laura unfairly criticized my marketing presentation.

    a. sore

    b. damaged

    c. hurt

    d. harmed

120. Next summer, I'm going to plant an herb _____ next to the house.

    a. foundation

    b. colony

    c. property

    d. garden

Reading—Part I

Read the passage. Then answer the questions on page 143 according to the information given in the passage.

A new study found that receiving loving attention in childhood promotes both emotional and physical well-being as adults. Researchers studied nearly 3,000 people age 25 to 74 and found that those who said their parents were nurturing had fewer incidences of chronic disease, including diabetes, high blood pressure, and arthritis. In contrast, the people who rated their parents poorly in such areas as "understanding problems and worries" or "giving time and attention when needed" also reported more illness. Experts suggest that children who receive greater support from their parents develop better coping mechanisms to deal with stress and other challenges in healthy ways.

Child psychologists recommend that parents spend quality time with their children and that they listen. For pre-school and elementary school-age children, it's important for parents to mix togetherness with time for their children to explore the world. These children want to exert their independence, but they still depend on their parents for a sense of security and reassurance. Parents need to participate in their children's lives both physically and emotionally. Middle school students who felt that their parents cared about them are better equipped to avoid health risks and behavioral problems. It's important for parents to schedule fun time together even if the children outwardly try to push them away, in part because the kids secretly want parental support and approval. By the time teenagers reach high school, they need to talk honestly with their parents about risky behavior and potential dangers. Through these simple and loving actions, parents can feel closer and more connected to their children while also promoting positive attitudes and behaviors so they are healthier as they grow older.

121. Who was interviewed for the study reported in this article?

    a. school-age children

    b. teenagers

    c. adults

    d. child psychologists

122. The main conclusion of the study is that

    a. parents who pay attention to their children suffer less from chronic diseases

    b. children who don't get enough attention are more easily stressed out as adults

    c. children who don't get along with their parents get sick easily

    d. children who speak honestly to their parents are healthier as they grow up

123. People who received more support from their parents as children

    a. tolerate stress better later in life

    b. are more independent as teenagers

    c. do not need security from their parents

    d. require less time with parents as they grow up

124. According to the passage, spending time with children is important

    a. to help them become independent

    b. to avoid risks and dangers

    c. to help them become independent

    d. to provide support and approval

125. What do child psychologists recommend parents to do with middle school children?

    a. explore the world around them

    b. push them away

    c. enjoy time together

    d. talk about diseases like diabetes and high blood pressure

126. What health benefits were found in the study?

    a. improved emotional and physical well-being

    b. several incidences of chronic disease

    c. understanding problems and worries

    d. increased independence and behavioral problems

Reading—Part II

Answer the questions on page 145 according to the information provided in the ads.

Indoor Waterpark

More than 20,000 sq. ft. of pools and water slides. Relax in a hot tub or just float along our specially designed lazy river. Enjoy lunch at Underwood's Underwater Cafe.

Waterpark daily admission fees: $10 for adults, $6 for children age 13–17, $4 for children age 5–12, free for children 4 and under. Thursdays, groups up to four for $10. Park open every day from 10 AM to 8 PM.

Cider Mill and Country Fair

Every fall, visit Underwood's Cider Mill and Country Fair. Free cider tasting every Sat. and Sun. from 1:00 to 5:00 PM. Daily tours of the orchard and mill.

Family fun with hay rides, cider and donuts, and a petting zoo open all day.

Admission:
Family rate: $15; Adults: $7;
Children (age 2–17): $4.

Cider Mill open from 11:00 AM to 8:00 PM.

Funland Arcade

The Underwood's Funland 3,000 sq. ft. arcade offers more than 100 of the best arcade games. The arcade has a great selection of prizes. Hours of operation: 8 AM to 11 PM.

Nightly Dinner Shows

Don't miss Tribute to the Stars! It's a fast-paced, 90-minute dinner show that features the music of country, classic rock, and rock and roll legends.

Nightly show at 8:00 PM Monday through Fridays. Weekends 4:00 PM matinee and 8:30 PM.

To complete your evening, add a limousine ride for only additional $20.

Underwood's Bakery and Sweet Shop

This month spend $15 on any bakery or food item and receive a FREE loaf of Michigan cherry bread. Excludes alcoholic beverages.

Receive 20% OFF Underwood's Private Label Apple Butter.

Store hours: 10 AM to 7 PM weekdays; 12 AM to 6 PM weekends.

127. It's 9:00 PM on Wednesday. What's open?

a. 1

b. 2

c. 4

d. 5

128. If you want to see a show, where do you go?

a. 2

b. 3

c. 4

d. 5

129. Where can you get a free gift with purchase?

a. 1

b. 3

c. 4

d. 5

130. Where can a family of four spend a fun day for $10?

a. 1

b. 3

c. 4

d. 5

131. Where can you win prizes?

a. 1

b. 2

c. 3

d. 5

132. Where can you take a tour?

a. 1

b. 2

c. 3

d. 4

133. Which places have discounts for families?

a. 1 & 3

b. 1 & 4

c. 2 & 3

d. 2 & 4

134. Which places are open at 7:00 PM on Saturday?

a. 1, 2, 4

b. 1, 2, 5

c. 2, 4, 5

d. 3, 4, 5

135. Which places have discounts?

a. 1, 2, 4

b. 1, 3, 5

c. 2, 4, 5

d. 3, 4, 5

136. Which places are open Sunday morning?

a. 1, 2, 3

b. 1, 2, 4

c. 2, 3, 4

d. 3, 4, 5

137. Which places serve food?

a. 1, 2, 3

b. 1, 3, 4

c. 2, 3, 4

d. 2, 4, 5

138. Which places have entry fees?

a. 1, 3, 4

b. 1, 4, 5

c. 2, 3, 4

d. 3, 4, 5

Reading—Part III

Read the questions on pages 147 and 148, and skim through the brochure to find the answers to the questions.

Have Fun in Farmington Hills

Underwood's Resort and Hotel offers 112 deluxe accommodations each with two beds and 45 new suites in beautiful Farmington Hills. The new family suites can accommodate from four to eight guests and include a fireplace, sitting area, microwave, and refrigerator. All suites have panoramic views of the hotel's spacious gardens and manicured lawns. Comfort and service are integral to a stay at Underwood's with all the amenities our guests have come to expect. To help you "keep fit" during your stay, visit our exercise room featuring stationary bikes, treadmills, and weight training equipment. Complimentary airport shuttle service. For reservations call 800-555-7000.

Promotions

Underwood's of Farmington Hills offers a variety of valuable overnight packages to choose from. We also have various promotions at different times of the year. Some of our most popular offerings are listed.

Join Underwood's Birthday Club!

Do you have a birthday to celebrate soon? If so, you can join our Birthday Club. Members receive a free family-style chicken dinner at Underwood's Restaurant during the month of their birthday, and more!

BIRTHDAY CLUB APPLICATION

First Name: _____

Last Name: _____

Address: _____

City: _____

State: _____ Zip Code: _____

Phone: _____

E-mail: _____

Birthdate: _____

Underwood's Plus Card Frequent Buyer Program

If you visit us often, you should get and use Underwood's Plus Card. Every time you complete ten purchases at any Underwood property, you will receive a certificate worth 10 percent of those ten purchases. Get your Underwood's Plus Card today, and start saving.

Underwood's Bread-of-the-Month Club

Annually, Underwood's Bakery of Farmington Hills bakes nearly one million loaves of bread that are served in its restaurant and award-winning bakery. Now you can share your favorite breads with friends and family by joining the Underwood's Bread-of-the-Month Club. For $60 a year, you get one loaf of fresh bread sent directly to your house at the beginning of each month.

Subscribe to Underwood's Sweet Shop

Enjoy fresh-baked goods and coffee from Underwood's Bakery all year long. Each month for a year, Underwood's will send you two sweet treats and specialty coffees to enjoy at your leisure. For $75, this makes a wonderful gift for all the special people in your life.

Underwood's Special Discounts

On the 15th of every month, receive 20 percent off one regular priced item at Underwood's Gift Shop, located on the lower level of Underwood's Restaurant.

This is only a practice test © 2006.

139. Who is likely to reserve a suite?

    a. a person traveling alone

    b. a couple on their honeymoon

    c. a group of six people

    d. a couple with one child

140. What are some features that make the suites special?

    a. fireplaces and kitchens

    b. two deluxe beds

    c. complimentary shuttle service

    d. they contain exercise equipment

141. How can guests keep fit?

    a. by taking the free shuttle

    b. by using the exercise equipment

    c. by viewing the spacious gardens

    d. by eating at the bakery

142. How can you get to Underwood's Hotel from the airport?

    a. Get a Frequent Buyer Program and you will get transportation coupons.

    b. Call for a reservation.

    c. Take the free bus.

    d. Take a taxi in the authorized area.

143. After subscribing to the Monthly Sweet Shop, what benefits do you get?

    a. baked goods and coffee

    b. a loaf of bread

    c. a special card

    d. a gift certificate

144. According to the information in the brochure, who should come to Farmington Hills?

    a. children to celebrate their birthdays

    b. senior citizens who want to rest

    c. families with children

    d. couples on their honeymoon

145. What do Birthday Club Members get?

    a. 20 percent off their meal

    b. two sweet treats

    c. a loaf of bread

    d. a free dinner

146. Who should get an Underwood's Plus Card?

    a. someone whose birthday is coming up soon

    b. someone who frequently eats bread

    c. someone who is visiting the hotel

    d. someone who often buys things at the hotel

147. What is the best way to save money at Underwood's?

    a. Join the Birthday Club, and visit on the 15th of your birthday month.

    b. Get the Underwood's Plus Card, and subscribe to the Monthly Sweet Shop.

    c. Join the Bread-of-the-Month Club and the Birthday Club.

    d. Join the Frequent Buyer Program, and go shopping on the 15th of the month.

148. If your sister likes cakes and cookies, what would be the best gift for her?

    a. a gift certificate

    b. a subscription to the sweet shop

    c. a bakery club membership

    d. a birthday club membership

149. Who should apply to the birthday club?

    a. people who like sweets

    b. people who like bread

    c. people who like chicken

    d. people who like coffee

150. When do club members get a free dinner?

    a. after making ten purchases with their card

    b. after joining the club

    c. during the month of their birthday

    d. on the 15th of every month

> End of GVR Test

Writing Test
INSTRUCTIONS

DO NOT BEGIN THIS SECTION UNTIL THE EXAMINER HAS READ THESE INSTRUCTIONS WITH YOU.

You may use pen or pencil for this section of the examination. First, print your name at the top of the separate writing paper. Then sign your name next to it. Next, print your date of birth. Then print the name of the test center and today's date.

For the Writing Section you will first read a short article. After you read the article, you can choose either Task 1 or Task 2. For Task 1 you will write a letter. For Task 2 you will write an essay. Do only ONE of these tasks.

You will have 30 minutes to write your letter or essay. You should write about one page. Start writing on the front of the paper. You may turn the paper over and continue on the back. If you wish, you may write an outline or notes in your test booklet. You may make any changes in the body of your letter or essay. Do not waste time re-copying your letter or essay to improve its appearance. Use your own words as much as possible. Do not copy a lot from the article given.

Your writing will be graded on how clearly you express your ideas. You must write on one of the two topics, or your paper will receive a failing grade. Use the appropriate format for a letter or essay. Be sure to write **1. Letter** or **2. Essay** on your writing paper before you begin.

If you have any questions during the Writing Section, raise your hand and a proctor will help you. Do you have any questions before you begin?

> End of the Writing Test

THE ANN ARBOR TIMES

The Ann Arbor City Council is considering a new law to protect the city's public libraries. In recent years, many books, CDs, and videos are lost or never returned. This has caused frustration of librarians and the people who wish to borrow these items. The new law will allow police to arrest someone who has kept library materials that are 60 days overdue or the third time something has not been returned on time.

Task 1. Letter

Write a letter to the editor of *The Ann Arbor Times.* What is your opinion of this new law? Explain why you think the City Council should adopt it or not. Start your letter, "Dear Editor."

Task 2. Essay

Public libraries provide the community with a collection of books and other services. With the Internet, some people do not think libraries are needed anymore. What are some advantages and disadvantages to having a public library? Explain your answer, giving specific examples.

Speaking Test

Situation

I am your friend, and I have a problem. Find out what the problem is and offer me some good advice.

Your Task

Look at the pictures and ask:

- Who is this person?
- What is the problem?
- What are the possible choices?
- What are the advantages and disadvantages of each choice?

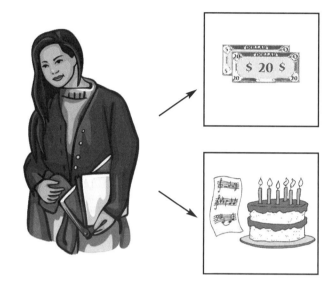

When you have all the information you need, you should offer some advice to help solve the problem. You can choose one of the solutions or create your own solution to the problem.

Remember

Use information you learn from asking questions to explain your final choice.

EXAMINER INFORMATION:

- Who is she? This is my good friend Jenny. She is 17.

- What is the problem? Tomorrow is her birthday. I want to get her a special present, but I have very little money. She has everything she wants. If I buy something I can afford, I'm afraid she may not like it. Then, I will have wasted my money.

Possible Options	Advantages	Disadvantages
Give her some money.	That's what she wants. She won't throw away my gift.	I really hate giving people money. I don't feel it's a real gift.
I can give her something that I make for her, like a birthday cake or a song.	It will be original, and she knows I spent time working on her present.	She may laugh at me or may not really think I'm a good friend.

Elaboration Questions

1. What gifts do you like to receive? What kind of gifts do you usually give your friends?

2. Do you like giving presents that you made yourself? What makes them special? If not, why not?

3. What do gifts say about the people who give them?

4. How important is the value of a gift from a friend?

Appendix
Student B Information

Unit 1, page 12

B. Your best friend spends all his time in front of a computer. Other than you, he only has cyber-friends who he chats with until late at night. He even has dates on-line. He says that he is happy this way and is not interested in going out of his room.

Options considered: (1) Join his chat room and tell him that you appreciate his friendship and want to spend time together, or (2) destroy his computer.

Join chat room:
Advantages: It may be more effective to talk to him this way, but you don't really enjoy chatting on-line.
Disadvantages: He may not accept having a conversation with you on-line.

Broken computer:
He won't be able to access the Internet, but he could go to Internet cafes to do it anyway.

Unit 2, page 28

B. You are worried about your cousin. He is a couch potato. He is 16 and spends most of the time in front of either the TV or the computer. He is at least 25 kilos overweight for his age.

Options considered: (1) Send him to a sports summer camp for a week, or (2) hire a personal trainer.

Summer camp:
Advantages: He can play different sports with more than 70 boys and girls his age.
Disadvantages: Cost is $250 for two weeks.

Personal trainer:
Advantages: He will receive individualized attention at the beach and a brand new gym.
Disadvantages: Cost is $400 for three hours per day for two weeks.

Unit 3, page 55

B. You are helping your teacher to choose a field trip for a class of 20 sixth graders (for a local school). The purpose of the field trip is to show the importance of having healthy eating habits.

Options considered: (1) Take the class to a picnic, or (2) take the class to a hospital.

Take the class to a picnic, and they prepare their own food:
Advantages: It's more engaging. It's a hands-on activity. Kids will enjoy preparing meals.
Disadvantages: It is potentially dangerous. We only have three hours for the field trip.

Take the class to a hospital, and talk to the nutritionist:
Advantages: It can be very informative. They can keep some brochures that discuss good eating habits.
Disadvantages: We have to pay a fee. The nutritionist is available only from 9 to 11 AM.

Unit 4, page 73

B. You have invited your boyfriend/girlfriend for dinner. You said you were an excellent cook, but you don't know how to cook at all. This is the first date.

Options considered: (1) Tell the truth, or (2) buy some food and say you prepared it.

To tell the truth:
Advantages: It's more honest to start a relationship telling the truth.
Disadvantages: It's hard to confess that you don't know how to cook.

To buy some food and say that you prepared it:
Advantages: You can impress your date with a fancy dinner.
Disadvantages: Sooner or later, your date will find out about your lie.

Unit 5, page 103

B. My friend loaned me money to buy new clothes to go to a party. Now he wants the money back, and I don't have anything to give him.

Options considered: (1) Get a part-time job on weekends at a fast-food restaurant, or (2) borrow money from another friend or a family member.

Get a part-time job:
Advantages: I will make my own money and get experience.
Disadvantages: I will have less time to study and spend with friends on weekends.

Borrow money:
Advantages: I may get the money faster.
Disadvantages: I will owe someone else money.

Unit 6, page 118

B. I know one of my friends is lying to his parents. He is 16 years old. He goes out with his girlfriend when his parents think he is at school.

Options considered: (1) Talk to my friend, or (2) talk to his parents.

Talk to my friend:
Advantages: He has always paid attention to what I have to say.
Disadvantages: His girlfriend never liked me and doesn't let him get close to me much anymore.

Talk to his parents:
Advantages: I am sure that his parents would be able to convince him to go to school.
Disadvantages: I am pretty sure that he would never talk to me again if I involve his parents.

Tapescripts

Unit 1 Listening Exercises

[Track 2]

After each conversation, a question is asked about what was heard. The possible answers to the question are shown as pictures. Circle the correct answer for each question. Remember that each conversation is heard only once. Conversations are not repeated.

1.   F: I'm so excited. Tomorrow, I'll be on a ten-hour flight to Asia.

    M: On long flights like that, it's important to walk up and down the aisles.

    F: Why?

    M: When you're inactive for long periods, you are more likely to form a large blood clot, and this can be dangerous.

    F: I heard that eating fruit, vegetables, and fish was supposed to reduce the risk.

    M: Drinking water is good, too. But it's still best to move around.

    F: You're right. I'll do that.

What will the woman do tomorrow?

2.   M: I haven't been able to sleep well for weeks. Now I have just missed another important deadline at work.

    F: It sounds like you are under a lot of pressure and stress. Have you tried exercising or getting a massage?

    M: No, but I tried doing yoga and meditating. Neither worked.

    F: How about seeing a career or life coach? My brother not only reduced his stress, but he also improved his work performance at the same time.

    M: That's great. It sounds better than exercise.

What will the man do next to relieve his stress?

3.   F: I've been feeling bloated lately. Usually when I drink plenty of plain water, the feeling goes away.

    M: Have you had fast food, soda, or coffee recently?

    F: Come to think of it, I have. Why?

    M: I read that chemicals found in these types of food and drink can cause bloating. Some doctors recommend eating parsley to get rid of the excess water.

    F: I knew parsley was good for freshening breath. Now, I'll be sure to eat some.

What caused the woman to feel bloated?

4. *M:* I had my annual check-up last week. My blood pressure is so high, my doctor gave me two months to reduce it or else she will prescribe medication at my next visit.

   F: That's terrible. I know that you have been under a lot of stress recently.

   M: Yeah. I've taken some stress management classes, but they weren't helping.

   F: Wait a minute. This morning on the radio, a nutritionist recommended eating three bananas a day to reduce blood pressure. Some people reported they lowered their blood pressure to normal levels within two to eight weeks.

   M: It can't hurt. I might be able to solve my problem by going to the grocery store instead of the drugstore.

What will the man do next to lower his blood pressure?

5. *F:* I can't believe Mom was on my case for staying up late studying again.

   M: Well, I'm sure she's worried that the lack of sleep will affect your health.

   F: I know. Now, she's telling me she's worried that I'm going to get diabetes. Is that crazy or what?

   M: Actually, no. The other night on television, there was a news report showing that people who got only six hours a night of sleep were nearly twice as likely to have diabetes than those who slept seven or more hours a night.

   F: Really! Well, after my exam tomorrow, I promise to get enough sleep every night.

What is worrying the woman's mother?

Unit 2 Listening Exercises

[Track 2]

After each conversation, a question is asked about what was heard. The possible answers to the questions are shown as pictures. Circle the correct answer for each question. Remember that each conversation is heard only once. Conversations are not repeated.

1. *M:* I want to start yoga, but the next class starts in two months.

   F: How about doing aerobics?

   M: I have a bad knee.

   F: There's a new water aerobics class. You'll get exercise, and it won't hurt your knee.

   M: I didn't bring a swimsuit today. I'll try it next week.

What will the man do next week?

2. *F:* I need to reduce my stress.

    M: Have you tried meditation? It's much better than exercise.

    F: No, I haven't. I've been taking medicine, and it hasn't been helping. Where do you go?

    What will the woman do next to reduce her stress?

3. *M:* I haven't been sleeping well at night.

    F: Do you drink coffee or tea at night?

    M: No, I don't have any caffeine after 10 AM. I don't have much stress, and I exercise daily.

    F: When do you exercise?

    M: Just before bedtime.

    F: Oh, no wonder. You've just gotten a boost of energy.

    What causes the man to sleep poorly?

4. *F:* Would you like an apple?

    M: Actually, I'd rather have an orange or a banana.

    F: There's a new study that found that eating apples helps you lose more weight for any type of diet.

    M: Really? Okay, on second thought, I will have one.

    What will the man eat?

5. *M:* How can you drink coffee before breakfast? I always start with juice.

    F: Last week, my friend told me that having coffee on an empty stomach can help keep my blood sugar level throughout the day.

    M: Really?

    F: Also, I found having it first makes me eat less.

    M: You've got me sold. I'll start now.

    What will the man have first today?

Mini-Test 1

Listening: Radio Interview

[Track 3]

Imagine you are listening to the radio. You are going to hear someone from a radio station interviewing one or more people at a special event. You will hear the interview in several parts. After each part, you will hear some questions. There are three answer choices for each question. You should select, from the three answer choices, the best answer to the question. If you want to, you may take notes as you listen.

Remember, after each section of the interview, you will hear some questions. On the test, the sections are separated by double lines. On the test, you will have 12 seconds to mark your answer by circling the letter of the best response.

[Track 4]

S1: This is Kelly Fountain. I'm here at the Community Health Fair. I am talking with a health expert, Dr. Michael Matthews. What do you want people to learn from attending this year's event?

S2: Kelly, it's important for everyone to learn how the body functions. By being able to separate myth from reality, people will actually be able to take better care of their health when they gain a solid understanding of how it all works.

1. Where are they?

2. Who is being interviewed?

3. What is one purpose of the event?

S1: What is one lesson people can learn?

S2: One interesting fact is that working out with weights also benefits the brain. A good sense of balance is a sign of brain strength, and working out with free weights helps develop better balance for someone over 45 years old. Just standing on one leg with eyes closed for more than 20 seconds is considered very good. Working out with free weights challenges the body because it stimulates neural pathways as body orientation and balance are maintained during this activity. Weight training machines do not have the same effect, since the weights are attached to the equipment and the body does not need to use its balancing abilities.

4. How does weight training affect the brain?

5. According to the speaker, what is an example of good balance?

6. According to the speaker, what happens when someone works out with free weights?

7. According to the speaker, why aren't weight machines effective?

S1: That's fascinating. What other myths do you address?

S2: Unfortunately, many people think that they can target exercise to "spot reduce" a specific problem area. For example, many people want to tone or flatten their abdomen. They think that if they just do hundreds of sit-ups every day, they will reduce the belly fat. However, that's not how the body works. If you want to build muscle in a particular area, the only way to target a trouble spot is through an overall program of aerobic exercise, resistance work, and a calorie-controlled diet.

8. What does the speaker mean by "spot reduce"?

9. According to the speaker, how does the body work?

10. According to the speaker, what is the best way to fix a trouble spot?

Unit 3 Listening Exercise

[Track 5]

After each conversation, a question is asked about what was heard. The possible answers to the questions are shown as pictures. Circle the correct answer for each question. Remember that each conversation is heard only once. Conversations are not repeated.

1. F: I'd like to have my coffee served with dessert.
   Where is the woman?

2. M: The nearest deli is three blocks down the street and in front of the library and across from the bus stop.
   Where is the man?

3. F: I'd like to order this chocolate cake for next Thursday with the words "Happy Birthday, William" written in white icing.
   Where is the woman?

4. M: It's such a beautiful day. I'm going to take my coffee break outside.
   Where is the man?

5. F: I've eaten lunch at my desk everyday. Today, I'm going out for a change. Would you like to join me?
   Where is the woman?

Unit 4 Listening Exercise

Listening: Radio Interview

[Track 6]

Imagine you are listening to the radio. You are going to hear someone from a radio station interviewing one or more people at a special event. You will hear the interview in several parts. After each part, you will hear some questions. There are three answer choices for each question. You should select, from the three answer choices, the best answer to the question. If you want to, you may take notes as you listen.

Remember, after each section of the interview, you will hear some questions. On the test, the sections are separated by double lines. On the test, you will have 12 seconds to mark your answer by circling the letter of the best response.

[Track 7]

F: This is Peggy Reeves. I'm here reporting live at the Third Annual Frugal Chef Competition in Seattle, Washington. With me here is the event Organizer, the Frugal Chef himself, Jeff Thompson. Jeff, what inspired you to create this cooking contest?

M: Well, Peggy, as you know, on my weekly cooking show, *The Frugal Chef*, I have found that people, not only in Seattle but all across the country, from Los Angeles to New York City and everyone in between like Denver and Detroit, that people in North America enjoy good food. However, they also appreciate a good value. The challenge for this competition is to create a new gourmet recipe using high-quality ingredients without spending more than $20 per dish. I have found the contestants to be extremely creative in their recipes.

1. Who is the woman?

2. Who is the man?

3. What is the event?

4. In which city does the event take place?

5. What is special about the event?

F: Jeff, we've heard that you added something new this year. Please tell us.

M: It's great. We were inspired by the Japanese cooking show *The Iron Wok*. This year, we are using a theme ingredient. It does not count toward the budget, but the contestants must use it in every dish. Plus, instead of just one dish, they will make as many dishes as they can to make a complete meal, including the appetizer and dessert.

6. Why did he change the format of the contest?

7. What is special about the theme ingredient?

8. How many dishes does each contestant make?

Mini-Test 2

Listening: Short Conversations

[Track 8]

This is a test of your ability to understand spoken English. You will hear short conversations. After you hear each conversation, you will be asked a question about what you heard. The answer choices in your test booklet are shown as pictures. Mark your answers by circling the letter of the best response.

1. *M:* How do you manage to work from home?
   F: Well, it wasn't always easy. At first, I tried working at the dining room table. Then, I tried the living room. Finally, I converted the guest bedroom into a home office.
   M: Was it expensive?
   F: Since I bought the furniture on sale, it wasn't too bad.

   In which room does the woman work at home?

2. *F:* I can't decide what to get Jane for her graduation present.
   M: Well, we know she loves chocolate!
   F: Yeah, but I want something that lasts. I want to give her a watch, but they are too expensive. I saw a great purse, but her mother just bought one for her.
   M: The department store has a great sale this weekend. Everything is 50 percent off.
   F: Great. I know exactly what I want to get.

   What will the woman buy?

3. *M:* We never seem to have any money left at the end of the month. Where does it all go?
   F: Well, we go out to see a movie every Friday night. During the week, I buy coffee in the morning and a snack in the afternoon. How about you?
   M: I buy a newspaper and coffee in the morning. Then I go out to lunch everyday.
   F: We could save money by watching TV on the weekend, having breakfast at home, or by packing lunches.
   M: I can't give up seeing movies, and I hate eating sandwiches or leftovers for lunch.

   What will they do to save money?

4. *F:* I can't decide how much to give my son for his weekly allowance. I was thinking about giving him one dollar for each year of his age.

   M: How old is he?

   F: He's 12 years old. I know that his friends get $20 a week, but I think that's too much.

   M: I read an article that suggests you give $5 at age 5 and then add $2 each year thereafter.

   F: Let's see, that would be $19. At that rate, I'd rather give him the same amount as the other kids.

   How much will the woman give her son each week?

5. *M:* We still haven't decided what to do for our family vacation. My wife loves cruises. But, now that the kids are older, I want them to see historic sites and visit museums.

   F: I thought you wanted to save money to buy a new car this year.

   M: It slipped my mind. I guess, we'll take it easy and have barbeques in the backyard after all.

   What will the man do for vacation?

Listening: Radio Interview

[Track 9]

Imagine you are listening to the radio. You are going to hear someone from a radio station interviewing one or more people at a special event. You will hear the interview in several parts. After each part, you will hear some questions. There are three answer choices for each question. You should select, from the three answer choices, the best answer to the question. If you want to, you may take notes as you listen.

Remember, after each section of the interview, you will hear some questions. On the test, the sections are separated by double lines. On the test, you will have 12 seconds to mark your answer to each question. Mark your answers by circling the letter of the best response.

[Track 10]

F: This is Meghan Nalley reporting to you live from the Family Financial Freedom Event at the Northville Community Center. Before me is Pat Dean, a financial advisor. Pat, what is special about this event?

M: Meghan, it is critical that families learn more than how to prepare a budget. To gain financial freedom, families need to understand their habits, both their thinking and their spending habits. Then, they need to look at their short-term and long-term goals.

This is important because gaining control over money helps decrease stress and enables families to efficiently plan for the future. Although many families may employ a financial advisor, everyone can start most of the planning on their own.

    6. What does Pat Dean do?

    7. How can families gain control over their finances?

    8. What does Pat suggest most families do to begin?

F: Pat, what happens if families don't start planning right away?

M: Most families leave their finances to chance. Without a plan, it is easy to lose control of spending and puts the family at risk of going into debt. One sure-fire way to make this happen is by wasting money. Many families spend a lot of money for things that are rarely used, such as expensive toys used once that then go into a closet and for hobbies that end up sitting on a shelf. This is something people could stop immediately.

    9. What is one danger of not having a plan?

    10. What is one habit that can be stopped immediately?

Unit 5 Listening Exercise

Listening: Short Conversations

[Track 11]

After each conversation, a question is asked about what was heard. The possible answers to the question are shown as pictures. Circle the correct answer for each question. Remember that each conversation is heard only once. Conversations are not repeated.

1.   *F:* I can't decide what to get my cousin for a wedding present.
    M: What have you looked at so far?
    F: Well, if I want to be practical, I will get her a toaster. However, I know she'd love to have a new coffee maker that can make cappuccino, too.
    M: Have you checked her registry at the department store?
    F: When I went last night, I saw that I could only afford a small flower vase.
    M: Hmm. You probably should get her what you think she'll really like.
    F: That's a good idea.

What will the woman give her cousin?

2. *M:* I'm worried. Recently, my son has been waking up and crying every night.

   F: Have you taken his temperature? Does he have a fever?

   M: Yes. He's a little warm, but he doesn't have a fever.

   F: Is he allergic to any food, or does he have a cold?

   M: He seems fine, no sneezing and no coughing.

   F: How old is he?

   M: He just turned six months last week.

   F: I think his teeth are coming in.

   M: Oh yeah, I remember reading that they are due about now. Thanks.

   What do they think is waking the baby at night?

3. *F:* I feel so bad. Every Thursday my daughter asks me to watch her play soccer after school, but there's a weekly staff meeting scheduled at the same time.

   M: Does she let you know that she's disappointed?

   F: No, but when I ask her if she wants to stop for some ice cream, she always says, "No, thanks." And she *loves* ice cream!

   M: What else does she like to do?

   F: She likes reading and shopping.

   M: How about taking her to the library on your next day off.

   F: That's a great idea. I've been wanting to go there for some time now.

   What did the daughter ask her mother to do?

4. *M:* I want to start saving money for my son's college education. But after paying all the bills, I never seem to have anything left to save.

   F: Do you have a budget or keep track of all of your expenses?

   M: No, I don't. How does that help?

   F: If you write down everything you spend money on for a month, you can then examine what's needed and what's not. Then you have your budget.

   M: Oh, I see.

   F: A budget helps you decide how much to save or spend on specific items. It helps you to decide what is important to spend money on in your life.

   M: Okay. I'll get a notepad to start my list from tomorrow.

   What will the man do tomorrow?

5. *F:* I can't understand why my brother and sister never seem to get along.

   M: What do they do?

   F: Every holiday, we have dinner at our parents' home, and they always get into a fight.

   M: Have you tried going out to eat at a restaurant instead?

F: Yes, it was incredibly embarrassing. They argued in public non-stop for two hours!

M: Has anyone talked to them about how the rest of you feel when they fight?

F: Hmm. I never thought about that. It can't hurt to do that.

What embarrassed the woman?

Unit 6 Listening Exercise

Listening: Radio Interview

[Track 12]

Imagine you are listening to the radio. You are going to hear someone from a radio station interviewing one or more people at a special event. You will hear the interview in several parts. After each part, you will hear some questions. There are three answer choices for each question. You should select, from the three answer choices, the best answer to the question. If you want to, you may take notes as you listen.

Remember, after each section of the interview, you will hear some questions. On the test, the sections are separated by double lines. On the test, you will have 12 seconds to mark your answer by circling the letter of the best response.

[Track 13]

S1: Good afternoon. Lily Sanders here reporting from the second Parents Expo held in Detroit. It's nearly the end of day one and, already more than 800 people have attended the two-day event to get information and ideas for being better parents. Tomorrow, they are expecting 900 more. Last year, nearly 1,200 people attended the First Expo. I'm here with the organizer, Christopher Grant. When you planned this event, who did you most want to attend?

S2: Lily, to be honest, I really wanted to have fathers, especially new fathers, come. I remember when I was a new father a few years ago. There were lots of books and information for women, but there was very little information for men who were about to become fathers. I remember being nervous and a little scared about taking care of a helpless infant. When I talked with other new fathers, we found that we had many fears in common.

1. How many people attended the first Parents Expo?

2. What day of the Expo is it?

3. Which group did the organizer want most to attend?

4. Why did the man want this group to attend the Expo?

5. What did he learn when he talked with new fathers?

S1: What seem to be the biggest fears that new fathers have?

S2: The greatest fear for many new fathers is not having the money to afford a new baby, especially if he is the sole wage earner. If money is tight, the family must keep track of every expense and live within a budget. The next biggest fear men have is about whether or not they will be good fathers. By understanding that it's impossible to become an expert overnight, a new father can relax and enjoy spending time with his baby. The more time he spends caring for the baby, the more comfortable he becomes and the more he enjoys being a parent.

6. What is the greatest fear for a new father?

7. Why is it important for a new father to relax?

8. What is the key for a new father to enjoy being a parent?

Full Test/Practice Test

Listening Test—Part I

[Track 14]

This is a test of your ability to understand spoken English. You will hear short conversations. After you hear each conversation, you will be asked a question about what you heard. The answer choices in your test booklet are shown as pictures. Mark your answers on the separate answer sheet. Do not write in the test booklet. Here is an example.

    M: What do you feel like having tonight?
    F: I met a client for lunch and had steak, so I'd prefer something light.
    M: Hmm. I had a hamburger and fries. . . .
    F: Roasted chicken with a large green salad would be healthy and easy to make.
    M: Sounds great. Just thinking about it is making me hungry.

What will they have for dinner?

The correct answer is *c* because they will make roasted chicken with a large green salad for dinner. The woman had steak for lunch. The man ate a hamburger and fries for his lunch.

You will hear each conversation only once; the conversations will not be repeated. Please be very quiet and listen carefully. Remember to mark all your answers on the separate answer sheet. You should mark A, B, or C. There are 30 questions in Part 1.

Do you have any questions before you begin?

[Track 15]

1. M: Are you getting Mom flowers for her birthday?
    F: No, I sent her some for Mother's Day. Why do you ask?
    M: I saw an ad for a nice arrangement.
    F: That sounds wonderful. I know Dad bought her earrings, and I got her a gift certificate to visit a spa.

    What will the man give his mother?

2. F: How are you planning to get to the convention?
    M: Flying is the fastest, but I thought it'd be fun to take the train.
    F: The train is nice, but it's actually faster to drive there yourself.
    M: I know, but parking at the hotel for a week can cost nearly as much as the airline tickets.
    F: I see your point. I think I'll join you.

    How will the woman travel?

3. M: Have you seen my glasses? I had them on when I drove home, but they got wet in the rain when I came inside.
    F: Did you check the garage, the dining room, or the bedroom?
    M: Now I remember. I was using a napkin from the table to dry them when the phone rang.

    Where are the man's glasses?

4. *F:* Where will you take Bobby this afternoon?

    M: Well, I wanted to go to the science museum, but it's closed today.

    F: How about the park? He loves the swings.

    M: It's expected to rain later today, so I thought he'd like to visit the library.

    F: Good idea; he'll enjoy looking at the science collection.

    Where will the man take Bobby?

5. *M:* Would you like to have chicken?

    F: We had it last night.

    M: I had a light lunch, so I'm hungry.

    F: I want something healthy, so no fast food.

    M: Hey, there's a special two-for-one dinner tonight.

    F: Great. Let's go!

    What will they have for dinner?

6. *F:* It's my nephew's birthday tomorrow, and I can't decide what to give him.

    M: What are your choices?

    F: His mom told me that he needs a new jacket. I know he's learning to play the guitar, but since he is so picky about his clothes, I thought that it may be best to just give him money.

    M: Money is convenient, but it won't last long.

    F: You have a point. In this case, I think his mother knows best.

    What will the woman give her nephew?

7. *M:* We missed you at the retirement party for Jean.

    F: I really wanted to be there, but I had to meet an important client for a lunch meeting.

    M: How did it go?

    F: Better than expected. I'm meeting him again tomorrow at his office to finalize the contract.

    Where was the woman earlier today?

8. *M:* Boy, am I tired!

    F: Did your baby keep you up all night?

    M: It wasn't that bad. She usually gets up at 5:30, but today she woke us up at 3:30 and did not go back to sleep until after I left for work at 7:30 this morning.

    F: I see. Would you like another cup of coffee?

    M: That'd be great. Thanks.

    When did the man get up this morning?

9. *F:* Where's Mark? It's noon already.

   M: Didn't he tell you? He's running late, so he'll join us here at the restaurant by 12:30.

   F: No, he didn't. Otherwise, I would've changed the reservation.

   M: It's just as well. Ted said he could come after all and will be here in ten minutes.

What time is it now?

10. *F:* I looked all through the supply closet and couldn't find any blue paper for the marketing reports.

   M: Did you ask the receptionist? I know she usually has some in her desk.

   F: I just did, but she ran out. Wait. Susan prepared the report last week; she may have some paper left.

   M: Come to think of it, I saw a stack on her filing cabinet this morning during our team meeting.

Where is the blue paper?

11. *M:* I can't find my glasses.

   F: Have you checked the bathroom sink?

   M: No, but I've checked the dresser next to the bed and the coffee table in the living room.

Where should the man look next?

12. *F:* The holiday decorations look great.

   M: Jenny told me they used special hooks to hang them this year.

   F: I remember last year the nails looked awful and the tape wasn't strong enough.

How are the decorations hung this year?

13. *M:* Would you like to see the new movie tonight?

   F: I'd love to, but since I have to finish my report for tomorrow, I can't spare the time.

   M: That's too bad. How about going out for some ice cream?

   F: That sounds great. But could we go tomorrow instead?

What will the woman do tonight?

14. *F:* What's your favorite sport?

   M: When I was a kid, I loved playing baseball. Then in college, I would swim everyday.

   F: What about now?

   M: I hardly exercise now, but I enjoy watching basketball.

What did the man do as a child?

15. *M:* Do we have anything to eat?

    F: The roast chicken will be ready in 20 minutes.

    M: I'm starving. Is there anything I can have now?

    F: Well, you can have some carrots or some canned fruit.

    M: On second thought, I'll wait for dinner.

    What will the man eat?

16. *F:* How are you getting to the picnic?

    M: I was planning to walk. But since it's raining, Bob offered to take me in his van. How are you going?

    F: I'm taking the bus.

    M: Why don't you join us? There's plenty of room.

    F: If it's okay with Bob, I think I will.

    How is the woman going to the picnic?

17. *M:* Where's Tony? We were supposed to meet in front of the elevator at noon. He's 15 minutes late.

    F: I know he was in a meeting at 11:00.

    M: I know that meeting ended a half an hour ago.

    What time did the man expect to meet Tony?

18. *M:* I heard that you're going camping this weekend.

    F: Yeah. We thought about going to the beach, but we couldn't get a hotel room.

    M: I know. We tried reserving a room, too. We're going to the swimming pool in the local park instead.

    What will the woman do this weekend?

19. *F:* How do you take your coffee? Would you like milk?

    M: No, thank you.

    F: How about some sugar?

    M: Just a little, thanks.

    What will the man have with his coffee?

20. *F:* I lost my gloves. Now my hands are freezing.

    M: Does your jacket have pockets?

    F: Yes, but they aren't deep enough for my hands.

    M: Here, you can use my mittens.

    F: Thanks.

    How will the woman keep her hands warm?

21. *M:* How would you like to pay for this?

    F: Oh, I forgot my checkbook, and I don't have enough cash.

    M: Would you like to charge it?

    F: I'd rather not, but I will.

How will the woman pay?

22. *F:* Do you have a newspaper?

    M: No, I just have a novel and a magazine for the plane.

    F: Let me stop in this store for a minute to buy one.

What does the woman want?

23. *M:* I'm so excited this will be my daughter's first music recital.

    F: Really. Does she play the piano?

    M: No. Actually, she started with the violin and then she switched to the flute.

What instrument will the man's daughter play?

24. *F:* Would you like fries with your sandwich?

    M: Do you have salad or fruit?

    F: We have both, but the salad will be a dollar extra.

    M: That's fine. It's worth the added cost.

What did the man order with his sandwich?

25. *M:* I thought the meeting was supposed to start at nine o'clock sharp.

    F: Didn't you get Greg's e-mail? He had another appointment and asked to have the meeting start an hour later.

    M: Hmm. I have another meeting from 10:30, so I can only stay for the first 15 minutes.

What time will Greg's meeting begin?

26. *F:* Which coat is yours?

    M: It's long and has a belt.

    F: Is it this dark-colored one?

    M: No, it's the other one with large light-colored buttons.

    F: I see it. I'll get it for you now.

Which is the man's coat?

27. *F:* I can't believe the day is only half over. We've been busy non-stop since the morning staff meeting.

   M: What have you been doing?

   F: We had a presentation for our biggest customer, then I had to finish writing the marketing report before lunch.

   M: Wow, that is a full morning!

How did the woman's day begin?

28. *M:* My doctor told me to lower my blood pressure or he will have to prescribe medication.

   F: What are you going to do?

   M: Well, I have been getting more exercise, but that is not enough.

   F: How about watching your salt intake? That's supposed to help.

   M: I haven't tried that yet.

What will the man likely do next to reduce his blood pressure?

29. *F:* Professor Williams asked me to bring the handouts for her class.

   M: Are they on her desk?

   F: No, she said they were in a folder on the table next to the copier.

   M: Oh, I put that folder on top of the file cabinet.

Where are Professor Williams' handouts?

30. *F:* Brrr. It's freezing today. Is it going to snow?

   M: No, it's freezing rain. It's not supposed to snow until tomorrow.

   F: I can't believe it was bright and sunny yesterday.

What is the weather like today?

End of Part I of the Listening Test

Listening Test—Part II

[Track 16]

Imagine you are listening to the radio. You are going to hear someone from a radio station interviewing three people at a special event.

- First, you will hear general information about this event.

- Then, you will hear from someone at the event.

- Next, you will hear from a psychologist.

- Finally, you will hear from a financial advisor.

You will hear the interviews in several parts. After each part, you will hear some questions. There are three answer choices for each question. You should select, from the three answer choices, the best answer to the question. If you want to, you may take notes in your test booklet as you listen.

Now you will hear the beginning of the first interview. For this part, there will not be any actual test questions. The questions that follow this part are examples only.

> S1: Hello, this is Robert Cooper from WELI. I'm reporting to you live from the fifth Secrets to Happiness Expo in Los Angeles just minutes away from the airport. I'm here with Sherry Brookwood, the Expo Organizer. How's it going?
>
> S2: Hi, Robert. Thanks for having me on your show. We expect a great turnout. Already we have more than 50,000 visitors! It's a lot of work, but I have a great team of people who are helping to make this event a huge success.

Example 1. Where are they now?
  A. at the airport
  B. at a radio station
  C. at an expo

The correct answer is C, at an expo.

Example 2. Who is the reporter interviewing?
  A. a team of people
  B. the organizer
  C. a visitor

The correct answer is B, the organizer.

Now, we will continue this interview. Remember, after each section of the interview you will hear some questions. In the test booklet, the sections are separated by double lines. On the test, you will have 12 seconds to mark your answer to each question. Mark your answers on the separate answer sheet. There will be 20 questions. Are there any questions before we begin?

[Track 17]

S1: This is Robert Cooper, and I'm reporting to you live from the fifth annual Secrets to Happiness Expo in Los Angeles. Last year's theme for the expo in New York City looked at health and well-being. This year the focus is on money. The next expo's theme has yet to be decided, but the location will be Chicago. I'm here with Sherry Brookwood, the Expo Organizer. Sherry, what is the connection between money and happiness?

S2: Thanks for having me here, Robert. Well, research shows us that although 81 percent of Americans say they are happy, six out of 10 worry about their finances. While those in households that make more than $50,000 a year are more likely to report being happy than those earning less, 70 percent of the people who feel in control of their finances say they are happy versus 22 percent of the people who do not feel like they have control over their money situation.

31. What was the theme of last year's Expo?

32. Where was last year's Expo?

33. How many Americans say they are happy?

34. What are households that make more than $50,000 a year more likely to report?

S1: That's very interesting. How important is it for a household to earn more than $50,000?

S2: Robert, it's interesting that most Americans think that they have to be a millionaire to be happy. The median household income is more than $42,000, so the $50,000 earning level isn't everything. There are many other factors. These are factors that anyone can change. Some are habits that people can adopt; others include information and behaviors that one can learn. By making these changes, the people who attend the Secrets to Happiness Expo can learn to feel better, happier, and more in control. This feeling of being in control over finances is literally one of the secrets to happiness.

35. How much money do Americans need to be happy?

36. What is important to know about the keys to happiness?

37. What can people learn at the Expo?

38. What is the median household income?

S1: Thanks, Sherry, for letting us in on the secret. Now, I will be talking with psychologist Dr. Lori Carr. Dr. Carr, what are the top three ways for people to gain control over their finances?

S2: It's amazing how lack of control leads to feelings of hopelessness, whereas gaining a sense of being in control can make one happy. What most people don't realize is that it really is the little things that make the biggest difference. The number one thing to do is be organized. It does not require a professional organizer or special furniture or filing systems. All it takes is creating a system that you understand, so that you can find any piece of paper that you need quickly and without any trouble. Being organized reduces frustration because items don't get lost and time isn't lost looking for them. The next one is to pay bills as they come in rather than wait to do it once a month. When the papers pile up, it eats up a big chunk of time to do it, plus it's awful to see a large sum of money going out to pay the bills all at once. The third action is to keep track of your money. Research shows that people who know exactly how much money is in their accounts are happier than those who don't.

39. What makes people feel hopeless?

40. What's the most important key to happiness?

41. What does a good system offer?

42. Why pay bills as they come in?

43. Why is it important to keep track of your money?

S1: Thank you, Dr. Carr, that was very informative. Now, let's switch to Diane Maxwell, a financial advisor. What are some simple things that you recommend to people that help them feel happier?

S2: Robert, one of the simplest things people can do is save at least 5 percent of their household income. There is a very strong relationship between saving and investing any amount and being happy, but the 5 percent mark makes the psychological difference for one to feel in control and, thus, happier. Another is to spend sensibly. It's the small money leaks, such as daily coffee, or magazines and snacks from a convenience store, that are the hardest to notice. Many people think they need these to be happy, but that changes once they see how much these indulgences cost over a year, such as the fact that spending $4 a day on specialty coffee can cost nearly $1,500 a year. When faced with the choice of saving $1,500 a year and having free coffee at work, many people will limit visits to the coffee shop to an occasional special treat.

44. What is the connection between saving money and being happy?

45. What amount of saving makes a strong psychological difference?

46. What is hard for people to notice?

47. Why would people prefer coffee made in the office?

S1: Wow! I didn't realize I could be saving so much money by brewing my own coffee for breakfast! Diane, are their any other secrets that you would like to share?

S2: It's important to have open communication with your spouse or partner about money. You can't be happy if you are constantly fighting about money. Beyond thinking about how your spouse may feel about money, it's important to create shared financial goals. Having a plan for saving makes decisions about spending much clearer. The final secret is to give away a portion of your money to charities and causes you believe in. Donating time or money leads to some of the strongest feelings of personal satisfaction and happiness of all.

48. Why is communication about money important?

49. What helps to make better spending decisions?

50. According to the speaker, what can make people the happiest?

End of the Listening Test

Answer Key

Unit 1: Good Vibes (pages 1–12)

6. Missing Phrases (page 4)

a. 1

b. 4

c. 2

d. 3

7. Skimming and Scanning (page 5)

1. Yes. Par 1

2. Yes. Par 3

3. Yes. Par 2 & 3

4. No

5. Yes. Par 4

6. No

7. Yes. Par 1

8. Yes. Par 1 & 5

8. Checking Comprehension (page 5)

1. d

2. b

3. c

4. d

9. Identifying Opinions (page 6)

Answers will vary. For open-ended exercises, we offer only model/sample answers. Teachers may choose to accept variations. Example:

	Author's Opinion	My Opinion
Laughter specialists think that happiness is more important than salary.	**Agree**/Disagree 1. reduces stress 2. increases job satisfaction	**Agree**/Disagree 1. 2.
We can learn a lot from young children.	**Agree**/Disagree 1. they laugh more 2. releasing tension	**Agree**/Disagree 1. playful 2. creative

10. Vocabulary: Word Forms (page 7)

Noun	Adjective	Synonym	Antonym (adjectives)
fear	fearful	*afraid, frightened*	*fearless*
anger	angry	upset, mad, upset	relaxed, calm, poised
worry	worried	tense, preoccupied	relaxed, unstressed
sadness	sad	unhappy, depressed, gloomy	happy, gay
creativity	creative	artistic	dull, boring

11. Vocabulary: Word Categories (page 7)

Answers will vary. Example:

Expressing Happiness	Expressing Sadness	Raising One's Voice	Making a Happy Face	Making a Sad Face
chuckle giggle gurgle laugh	cry weep wail	holler shout yell screech	smile grin	frown pout

12. Grammar: Placement of Adverbs (page 8)

1. has been recently questioned/has recently been questioned/has been questioned recently
2. is being conducted nowadays
3. have actually found
4. was not publicly recognized
5. is now considered

13. Sentence Completion (page 8)

Answers will vary.

15. Listening: Short Conversations (page 10)

1. C
2. C
3. B
4. C
5. C

Unit 2: Stress and Fitness (pages 13–28)

7. Checking Comprehension (page 18)

1. b
2. a
3. d
4. c
5. b
6. d

8. Checking Comprehension (page 20)

1. b
2. a
3. d
4. a
5. a
6. b

9. Vocabulary (page 22)

1. supportive
2. relieved
3. achievement
4. deprived
5. optimal
6. retreat
7. range
8. reach/achieve
9. surroundings
10. peak

10. Grammar: Expressing Contrast (page 23)

2. Although
3. In spite of
4. though/however
5. but/though/although
6. Although
7. but/although
8. However

11. Grammar: Subjunctive Forms (page 24)

Answers will vary. Examples:

1. join them on the second week of their honeymoon
2. Billy have monthly medical checkups to see how he is doing with his allergy.
3. they start a fitness program during their lunch hour and invite all employees to bring healthier food and to get together for an exercise class.
4. should go out and meet more people.
5. someone participate in the next competition and to have practice twice as often for the next two weeks.

13. Listening: Short Conversations (page 26)

1. C
2. A
3. C
4. A
5. A

Mini-Test 1 (pages 29–40)

1. a	11. a	21. a	31. a
2. b	12. a	22. c	32. b
3. b	13. c	23. b	33. b
4. c	14. b	24. c	34. d
5. b	15. b	25. d	35. b
6. a	16. b	26. b	36. c
7. c	17. b	27. a	37. c
8. a	18. c	28. a	38. a
9. c	19. c	29. d	39. d
10. b	20. c	30. b	40. a

Unit 3: Eating "Good" Stuff (pages 41–55)

5. Fill in the Blank (page 43)

a. 4

b. 2

c. 3

d. 1

6. Skimming (page 45)

1. 59-year-old heart patient

2. a hospital spokesperson

3. a senior vice president of a national hamburger franchise

4. the head of the national association of health care administrators

7. Understanding Main Ideas (page 45)

1. Utah's most famous hospital

2. Moving fast-food franchises out of the hospital

3. A trend that raises awareness and connects good nutritional choices with wellness

4. Do we serve healthy foods because we work in a health-care facility, or do we serve what the customers really want to eat?

8. Checking Comprehension (page 46)

1. b

2. b

3. a

4. b

5. b

6. d

7. b

8. d

9. Vocabulary: Synonyms (page 48)

a. stared

b. fat

c. physician

d. prominent

e. facility

10. Vocabulary: Word Forms   (page 48)

Noun	Adjective	Antonym (for adjectives)
health	healthy	unhealthy
awareness	aware	unaware
balance	balanced	unbalanced
temptation	tempting	untempting
disappointing	disappointing	pleasing

11. Vocabulary: Business Terms (page 49)

1. franchise
2. royalties
3. fee
4. vendors
5. proceeds
6. revenue
7. lease
8. budget

12. Grammar: Relative Clauses (page 50)

Answers will vary.

13. Grammar: Identifying and Correcting Errors (page 51)

I   1. *do* should be *does*
I   2. *who* should be *that/which*
C   3.
I   4. *is* should be *be*
I   5. *However* should be *Although*

15. Listening: Conversations (page 53)

1. b
2. a
3. a
4. b
5. b

Unit 4: Eating to Live or Living to Eat (pages 56–74)

2. Creative Uses for Food (page 57)

1. Salt: removing wine stains
2. Carrots: carve into flowers as a garnish
3. Rice: keeping food dry
4. Olive Oil: skin moisterizer
5. Vinegar: mix with baking soda to clean sink pipes

3. Categories in a Supermarket (page 57)

Meat	Dairy	Beverages	Snacks	Kitchenware
chicken	cheese	coffee	cookies	can opener
beef	yogurt	wine	potato chips	chopping board
eggs	milk	soda pop	crackers	mixing bowl
pork	butter	tea	nuts	pot holder
fish			chocolate chips	
			candy	

4. Scanning for Information (page 59)

1. a
2. b
3. c
4. d
5. b
6. c
7. d
8. a
9. a
10. d
11. d
12. a

5. Matching (page 61)

1. e
2. b
3. f
4. a

6. Checking Comprehension (page 63)

1. b	7. a
2. d	8. b
3. c	9. c
4. c	10. d
5. a	11. d
6. d	12. b

7. Vocabulary: Word Categories (page 66)

Answers will vary but may include the following:

Places Where You Can Eat	breads	meals	textures	condiments
cafeteria coffee shop	bagel bun donut	brunch snack	chewy crispy crunchy	syrup sauce dressing

8. Grammar: Comparative Sentences (page 66)

Answers will vary. Some examples:

1. Some actors are more famous than most presidents.
2. My sister is more friendly than my brother.
3. Pizza is easier to make than pasta.
4. My aunt drives more carefully than my uncle.
5. The accountant is more honest than the manager.
6. My friends are more enthusiastic than my parents.
7. Dogs are happier than cats.
8. Fish are quieter than birds.

9. Grammar: Verbal Phrases (page 67)

1. a
2. b
3. c
4. b
5. c
6. b
7. a
8. a

10. Grammar: Verbal Phrases (page 69)

1. Designed
2. Serving
3. Having instructed
4. having
5. not to have remembered
6. becoming
7. to leave
8. bring

13. Listening: Radio Interview (page 71)

1. c
2. a
3. a
4. b
5. b
6. b
7. a
8. c

Mini-Test 2 *(pages 75–86)*

Listening: Short Conversations	Grammar	Vocabulary	Reading
1. c	11. c	21. b	31. b
2. b	12. d	22. b	32. a
3. b	13. d	23. b	33. c
4. c	14. b	24. a	34. a
5. c	15. b	25. d	35. d
Listening: Radio Interview	16. a	26. d	36. d
	17. b	27. a	37. a
6. c	18. b	28. c	38. c
7. b	19. a	29. c	39. a
8. b	20. a	30. d	40. c
9. b			
10. c			

Unit 5: Ready to Handle Money? *(pages 87–103)*

5. Scanning for Information (page 90)
1. a small sum
2. a larger sum

6. Checking Comprehension (page 91)
1. c
2. d
3. a
4. d
5. b
6. b
7. c

8. Vocabulary: Matching (page 94)
1. d
2. e
3. g
4. h
5. b
6. f
7. c
8. a

9. Grammar: Phrasal Verbs (page 94)
1. b
2. c
3. d
4. a
5. c

6. b
7. c
8. a

10. Grammar: Conditional Clauses (page 96)
Answers will vary.

11. Grammar: Adverbial Clauses (page 97)
Answers will vary.

12. Grammar: Indefinite Pronouns and Quantifiers (page 98)
1. d
2. c
3. b
4. a
5. a
6. d

13. Sentence Completion (page 99)
Answers will vary.

15. Listening: Short Conversations (page 101)
1. b
2. c
3. c
4. c
5. b

Unit 6: *Family and Relationships (pages 104–118)*

4. Checking Comprehension (page 107)

1. c
2. b
3. b
4. b
5. a

5. Scanning for Information (page 109)

1. d
2. c
3. b
4. d
5. a
6. b
7. b
8. b
9. a
10. d

6. Vocabulary: Associated Words (page 111)

a. sculpt; *done on flat surface*
b. lecture; *refers to older people usually*
c. exit; *for entering a museum*
d. lease; *owning property*
e. bike; *used only for babies*
f. sibling; *siblings can be adults*

7. Grammar: Review of Verb Tenses and Modal Auxilaries (page 111)

1. d
2. c
3. b
4. c
5. b
6. a
7. c
8. d
9. c

8. Grammar: Discourse Markers (page 113)

Answers will vary.

9. Grammar: Prepositions (page 114)

1. in, on
2. in, for/at
3. of
4. with, of
5. on
6. into, for
7. between
8. from, after

10. Grammar: Phrasal Verbs (page 114)

Answers will vary.

12. Listening: Radio Interview (page 116)

1. c
2. b
3. b
4. b
5. a
6. b
7. b
8. a

ECCE Full Test/Practice Test (pages 119–152)

1. a	39. a	77. b	115. a
2. c	40. c	78. c	116. d
3. c	41. b	79. d	117. c
4. b	42. a	80. d	118. b
5. c	43. a	81. b	119. c
6. b	44. c	82. b	120. d
7. b	45. a	83. a	121. c
8. a	46. c	84. d	122. b
9. a	47. b	85. c	123. a
10. c	48. a	86. b	124. d
11. a	49. b	87. d	125. c
12. a	50. c	88. a	126. a
13. b	51. d	89. c	127. b
14. a	52. a	90. d	128. b
15. a	53. b	91. a	129. d
16. b	54. a	92. c	130. a
17. a	55. b	93. b	131. b
18. a	56. a	94. a	132. d
19. b	57. a	95. b	133. b
20. c	58. c	96. d	134. a
21. c	59. c	97. d	135. b
22. a	60. a	98. b	136. b
23. c	61. b	99. b	137. b
24. b	62. a	100. a	138. a
25. b	63. b	101. b	139. c
26. b	64. b	102. d	140. a
27. a	65. a	103. d	141. b
28. c	66. d	104. a	142. c
29. c	67. a	105. b	143. a
30. b	68. c	106. c	144. c
31. c	69. c	107. d	145. d
32. a	70. a	108. d	146. d
33. c	71. a	109. b	147. a
34. a	72. c	110. a	148. b
35. c	73. a	111. c	149. c
36. a	74. b	112. b	150. c
37. b	75. d	113. a	
38. b	76. b	114. d	